Helen Hayes

Helen Hayes

MARY KITTREDGE

CHELSEA HOUSE PUBLISHERS

NEW YORK · PHILADELPHIA

Chelsea House Publishers
EDITOR-IN-CHIEF Nancy Toff
EXECUTIVE EDITOR Remmel T. Nunn
MANAGING EDITOR Karyn Gullen Browne
COPY CHIEF Juliann Barbato
PICTURE EDITOR Adrian G. Allen
ART DIRECTOR Maria Epes
MANUFACTURING MANAGER Gerald Levine

American Women of Achievement
SENIOR EDITOR Richard Rennert

Staff for HELEN HAYES
TEXT EDITOR Marian W. Taylor
COPY EDITOR Philip Koslow
DEPUTY COPY CHIEF Mark Rifkin
EDITORIAL ASSISTANT Nicole Claro
PICTURE RESEARCHER Michèle Brisson
ASSISTANT ART DIRECTOR Loraine Machlin
DESIGNER Debora Smith
LAYOUT Design Oasis
PRODUCTION MANAGER Joseph Romano
PRODUCTION COORDINATOR Marie Claire Cebrián
COVER ILLUSTRATOR Melinda Kingsley

5 7 9 8 6

Library of Congress Cataloging-in-Publication Data

Kittredge, Mary
  Helen Hayes/by Mary Kittredge.
    p.   cm.—(American women of achievement)
  Bibliography: p.
  Includes index.
  Summary: An illustrated biography of the celebrated actress.
  ISBN 1-55546-656-7
      0-7910-0436-8 (pbk.)
  1. Hayes, Helen, 1900– . 2. Actors—United States—
Biography—Juvenile literature. [1. Hayes, Helen, 1900–
  2. Actors and actresses.] I. Title. II. Series.
PN2287.H35K58   1988
792'.028'0924—dc19   87-37585
[B]   CIP
[92]   AC

CONTENTS

AMERICAN WOMEN OF ACHIEVEMENT

Abigail Adams
women's rights advocate

Jane Addams
social worker

Louisa May Alcott
author

Marian Anderson
singer

Susan B. Anthony
woman suffragist

Ethel Barrymore
actress

Clara Barton
founder of the American Red Cross

Elizabeth Blackwell
physician

Nellie Bly
journalist

Margaret Bourke-White
photographer

Pearl Buck
author

Rachel Carson
biologist and author

Mary Cassatt
artist

Agnes de Mille
choreographer

Emily Dickinson
poet

Isadora Duncan
dancer

Amelia Earhart
aviator

Mary Baker Eddy
founder of the Christian Science church

Betty Friedan
feminist

Althea Gibson
tennis champion

Emma Goldman
political activist

Helen Hayes
actress

Lillian Hellman
playwright

Katharine Hepburn
actress

Karen Horney
psychoanalyst

Anne Hutchinson
religious leader

Mahalia Jackson
gospel singer

Helen Keller
humanitarian

Jeane Kirkpatrick
diplomat

Emma Lazarus
poet

Clare Boothe Luce
author and diplomat

Barbara McClintock
biologist

Margaret Mead
anthropologist

Edna St. Vincent Millay
poet

Julia Morgan
architect

Grandma Moses
painter

Louise Nevelson
sculptor

Sandra Day O'Connor
Supreme Court justice

Georgia O'Keeffe
painter

Eleanor Roosevelt
diplomat and humanitarian

Wilma Rudolph
champion athlete

Florence Sabin
medical researcher

Beverly Sills
opera singer

Gertrude Stein
author

Gloria Steinem
feminist

Harriet Beecher Stowe
author and abolitionist

Mae West
entertainer

Edith Wharton
author

Phillis Wheatley
poet

Babe Didrikson Zaharias
champion athlete

CHELSEA HOUSE PUBLISHERS

"REMEMBER THE LADIES"

MATINA S. HORNER

Remember the Ladies." That is what Abigail Adams wrote to her husband, John, then a delegate to the Continental Congress, as the Founding Fathers met in Philadelphia to form a new nation in March of 1776. "Be more generous and favorable to them than your ancestors. Do not put such unlimited power in the hands of the Husbands. If particular care and attention is not paid to the Ladies," Abigail Adams warned, "we are determined to foment a Rebellion, and will not hold ourselves bound by any Laws in which we have no voice, or Representation."

The words of Abigail Adams, one of the earliest American advocates of women's rights, were prophetic. Because when we have not "remembered the ladies," they have, by their words and deeds, reminded us so forcefully of the omission that we cannot fail to remember them. For the history of American women is as interesting and varied as the history of our nation as a whole. American women have played an integral part in founding, settling, and building our country. Some we remember as remarkable women who—against great odds—achieved distinction in the public arena: Anne Hutchinson, who in the 17th century became a charismatic religious leader; Phillis Wheatley, an 18th-century black slave who became a poet; Susan B. Anthony, whose name is synonymous with the 19th-century women's rights movement and who led the struggle to enfranchise women; and, in our own century, Amelia Earhart, the first woman to cross the Atlantic Ocean by air.

These extraordinary women certainly merit our admiration, but other women, "common women," many of them all but forgotten, should also be recognized for their contributions to American thought and culture. Women have been community builders; they have founded schools and formed voluntary associations to help those in need; they have assumed the major responsibility for rearing children, passing on from one generation to the next the values that keep a culture alive. These and innumerable other contributions, once ignored, are now being recognized by scholars, students, and the public. It is exciting and gratifying to realize that a part of our history that was hardly acknowledged a few generations ago is now being studied and brought to light.

In recent decades, the field of women's history has grown from obscurity to a politically controversial splinter movement to academic respectability, in many cases mainstreamed into such traditional disciplines as history, economics, and psychology. Scholars of women, both female and male, have organized research centers at such prestigious institutions as Wellesley College, Stanford University, and the University of California. Other notable centers for women's studies are the Center for the American Woman and Politics at the Eagleton Institute of Politics at Rutgers University; the Henry A. Murray Research Center for the Study of Lives, at Radcliffe College; and the Women's Research and Education Institute, the research arm of the Congressional Caucus on Women's Issues. Other scholars and public figures have established archives and libraries, such as the Schlesinger Library on the History of Women in America, at Radcliffe College, and the Sophia Smith Collection, at Smith College, to collect and preserve the written and tangible legacies of women.

From the initial donation of the Women's Rights Collection in 1943, the Schlesinger Library grew to encompass vast collections documenting the manifold accomplishments of American women. Simultaneously, the women's movement in general and the academic discipline of women's studies in particular also began with a narrow definition and gradually expanded their mandate. Early causes such as woman suffrage and social reform, abolition and organized labor were joined by newer concerns such as the history of women in business and the professions and in politics and government; the study of the family; and social issues such as health policy and education.

Women, as historian Arthur M. Schlesinger, jr., once pointed out, "have constituted the most spectacular casualty of traditional history.

They have made up at least half the human race, but you could never tell that by looking at the books historians write." The new breed of historians is remedying that omission. They have written books about immigrant women and about working-class women who struggled for survival in cities and about black women who met the challenges of life in rural areas. They are telling the stories of women who, despite the barriers of tradition and economics, became lawyers and doctors and public figures.

The women's studies movement has also led scholars to question traditional interpretations of their respective disciplines. For example, the study of war has traditionally been an exercise in military and political analysis, an examination of strategies planned and executed by men. But scholars of women's history have pointed out that wars have also been periods of tremendous change and even opportunity for women, because the very absence of men on the home front enabled them to expand their educational, economic, and professional activities and to assume leadership in their homes.

The early scholars of women's history showed a unique brand of courage in choosing to investigate new subjects and take new approaches to old ones. Often, like their subjects, they endured criticism and even ostracism by their academic colleagues. But their efforts have unquestionably been worthwhile, because with the publication of each new study and book another piece of the historical patchwork is sewn into place, revealing an increasingly comprehensive picture of the role of women in our rich and varied history.

Such books on groups of women are essential, but books that focus on the lives of individuals are equally indispensable. Biographies can be inspirational, offering their readers the example of people with vision who have looked outside themselves for their goals and have often struggled against great obstacles to achieve them. Marian Anderson, for instance, had to overcome racial bigotry in order to perfect her art and perform as a concert singer. Isadora Duncan defied the rules of classical dance to find true artistic freedom. Jane Addams had to break down society's notions of the proper role for women in order to create new social institutions, notably the settlement house. All of these women had to come to terms both with themselves and with the world in which they lived. Only then could they move ahead as pioneers in their chosen callings.

Biography can inspire not only by adulation but also by realism. It helps us to see not only the qualities in others that we hope to emulate but also, perhaps, the weaknesses that made them "human." By helping us identify with the subject on a more personal level they help us to feel that we, too, can achieve such goals. We read about Eleanor Roosevelt, for example, who occupied a unique and seemingly enviable position as the wife of the president. Yet we can sympathize with her inner dilemma: an inherently shy woman who had to force herself to live a most public life in order to use her position to benefit others. We may not be able to imagine ourselves having the immense poetic talent of Emily Dickinson, but from her story we can understand the challenges faced by a creative woman who was expected to fulfill many family responsibilities. And though few of us will ever reach the level of athletic accomplishment displayed by Wilma Rudolph or Babe Zaharias, we can still appreciate their spirit, their overwhelming will to excel.

A biography is a multifaceted lens. It is first of all a magnification, the intimate examination of one particular life. But at the same time, it is a wide-angle lens, informing us about the world in which the subject lived. We come away from reading about one life knowing more about the social, political, and economic fabric of the time. It is for this reason, perhaps, that the great New England essayist Ralph Waldo Emerson wrote, in 1841, "There is properly no history: only biography." And it is also why biography, and particularly women's biography, will continue to fascinate writers and readers alike.

Helen Hayes

Costumed as the young queen of England, Helen Hayes plays a scene from Victoria Regina, *the 1935 drama that proved to be one of her greatest triumphs.*

ONE

"The Best I Could Deliver"

The stately, silver-haired woman raised her hand commandingly. Overhead lights struck sparks from her jeweled fingers and glinted off her sweeping black satin gown. Diminutive but regal from her deeply lined face to her high-buttoned black boots, Queen Victoria of England was about to speak her mind. Then she stopped suddenly.

Actress Helen Hayes sighed impatiently. She was 35 years old; Victoria was 80. Costume, makeup, hair coloring, and cheek padding were not enough. She did not *feel* like an 80-year-old woman. This dress rehearsal for *Victoria Regina*, held in the fall of 1935, followed weeks of intensive preparation. The play would soon open on Broadway, but Hayes had not yet captured her character.

It was Hayes's job to personify Victoria, Britain's monarch from 1837 to 1901, from young womanhood through

old age. Playing the queen as a young woman presented no problem to the seasoned actress, but playing her as a great-grandmother was another matter. So far, the frustrated Hayes felt, she had been merely imitating the aging Victoria. "I was awful," she recalled later. She knew she could make an audience believe in her character only if she *became* that character.

Doubtful about playing someone so much older than herself, Hayes had tried to persuade British playwright Laurence Housman to end the story before Victoria entered old age. Housman had refused, insisting that Hayes could find a way to solve the problem. Because she loved the play, Hayes had finally agreed to take the part. Now it was too late to change her mind.

At 35, Hayes was a 30-year theatrical veteran. She had first appeared on the stage at the age of 5; since then, she had given thousands of performances in more than 50 plays. Although her heart belonged to the theater, she had also triumphed in movies, appearing in several silent films and winning the 1931–32 Academy Award for her performance in a "talking picture," *The Sin of Madelon Claudet*. Now, in 1935, Hayes was among the best-known and most popular actresses in the English-speaking world. *Victoria Regina* would be the climax of her career thus far—if she could do it.

Hayes did not expect miracles: "It is vanity," she wrote later, "to believe that your acting will be touched by the divine more than once or twice." But she did hope to "achieve excellence" and to ensure that her audiences would "never be disappointed and never bored." Victoria had turned out to be an even bigger challenge than she had anticipated. On this autumn day in New York, Hayes's normally buoyant spirits flagged as she left the theater. "You go home," she later wrote of such a day, "with your feet aching and your back and your head—and usually your soul—aching, because every muscle in you has been strained toward that goal of capturing the essence of the character you are trying to interpret."

That night, her mind still on Victoria, Hayes tried to sleep. "I was in a panic," she recalled, "blinded and confused." Then she suddenly thought of "Graddy," the grandmother who had helped bring her up. "As I lay in bed," she recalled afterward, "my Graddy Hayes marched across my vision. There she was and there was Victoria. She settled down inside of me and took

A portrait of the historical queen, shown on the Victoria Regina *program, underscores the startling accuracy of Hayes's re-creation.*

over." As a very young girl, Hayes's English-born grandmother had watched Victoria's 1840 wedding procession, cheering as the 21-year-old queen rode by with her handsome bridegroom, Prince Albert. Graddy Hayes had often told her granddaughter stories about the British ruler, whom she admired enormously.

Hayes, who was born in 1900, later wrote, "The queen died when I was a year old, but for ten years after that, my

Hayes, 35, portrays Queen Victoria at 80. Most theatergoers, including Victoria's own granddaughter, found the actress utterly convincing as the elderly monarch.

grandmother wore the bonnet with the black egret [feather] that was [Victoria's] fashion and conducted herself like her idol." Once she had made the connection between grandmother and queen, Hayes's problems with her role ended. From that point on, she noted later, "I never saw anything but my Graddy in my mind's eye every night I played the part."

When it opened at Manhattan's Broadhurst Theatre in late 1935, *Victoria Regina*—and its star—attracted a standing-room-only crowd. Theater patrons rose to cheer Hayes's entrance as the young queen; she seemed to float onto the stage, her dark hair pulled smoothly back, her slim body sheathed in a long white dress. As one act succeeded another, Hayes fans demonstrated their approval with waves of applause. But the real test of her abilities was yet to come.

As the play neared its conclusion, the curtain rose on an 80-year-old Queen Victoria. Sitting silently at stage center, she wore a somber black dress. Her hair was gray, her cheeks puffy, her movements stiff. Even her eyes appeared dimmed by age. Still, she seemed to radiate iron-willed strength. Many theatergoers later said they assumed Hayes had been replaced by an older actress for the play's finale—until she spoke. Then, realizing that this uncompromising old woman was the same lithe and graceful actress they had watched from the beginning, the audience gave her a standing ovation.

Theater critics, too, greeted the play with a roar of acclaim. As Victoria,

Catherine Hayes Brown proudly watches her daughter's first-night performance as Victoria.

asserted reviewers, Hayes had delivered the performance of a lifetime. "Miss Hayes succeeds in being a queen without ever forgetting she is a woman," observed critic John Mason Brown. She had the "artistic perception," he added, "to realize that what makes a queen a queen is not the costume she wears . . . but the blood coursing through her veins and the spirit born of it."

Another prominent drama critic, Brooks Atkinson of the *New York Times*, called Hayes's Victoria a "masterpiece." The actress, he said, "made the theater larger than life. . . . She made a living person out of a myth." Fellow actress Lillian Gish announced that Hayes had been "wonderful as

Victoria"; actor John Gielgud said she had been "superb—exceedingly witty as well as touching, particularly in the scenes with Albert [played by a young actor named Vincent Price] and the two final scenes as the old lady."

For Hayes, even more satisfying than the critics' praises were the words she heard from Victoria Eugénie Julia Ena, former queen of Spain and granddaughter of Britain's queen Victoria. After attending a performance of *Victoria Regina*, the royal playgoer invited the actress to tea. "How did you ever learn so many things about my grandmother?" she asked. "Why, you laugh like her and talk like her, and who told you of that impatient little shrug she made if anyone tried to sympathize with her or help her when she was old?" Hayes smiled. "I didn't tell her,"

she wrote later, "I was just doing my grandmother.... They were simply two old ladies with the same inner spirit. Using one made the other come alive."

Helen Hayes played Victoria for another 969 performances, making *Victoria Regina* one of the greatest dramatic hits in Broadway history. Her characterization seemed to impress everyone who saw it. British playwright Noël Coward called her the "greatest living actress," and *Life* magazine, in its first issue, pronounced her "the most far-reaching and influential" of all American actresses. "She is entitled to be known," said *Life*, "as our First Actress." Hayes's reaction to the extravagant praise was characteristically understated: "I brought out the best I could deliver," she said.

The future First Lady of the American Theater wears a diaper and a smile for this formal portrait, made when she was nine months old.

TWO

"My Destiny Seemed Assured"

Helen Hayes Brown, the only child of Catherine and Frank Brown, was born in Washington, D.C., on October 10, 1900. Her mother had always loved the theater and still dreamed of becoming a star, but her traveling-salesman father shared none of his wife's craving for theatrical glamour. Frank Brown was a placid, soft-spoken man whose dreams extended no further than his family, his home, and his garden.

Helen Hayes discussed her family in her 1968 autobiography, *On Reflection*. Her mother, she said, had married to escape from her own father, Patrick Hayes. A tyrant given to violent displays of temper, Hayes had been known to hurl a carefully prepared meal to the floor if some detail displeased him. When he was in an especially bad humor, his wife would dip into her household money and take her daughter to the theater.

Catherine Estelle Hayes—"Essie" to her family and friends—came to regard the theater as a place of wonder, a sanctuary from harsh reality. By the time she reached her teenage years, she had decided to follow in the footsteps of her great-aunt Catherine, a popular Irish singer known as the Swan of Erin. To reach her goal, Hayes needed to free herself from her father's iron control, so she married Frank Brown. She never intended to become an ordinary suburban housewife. Essie Brown planned to light up the stage.

Francis Van Arnum (Frank) Brown had expected a conventional married life: He would make his sales trips, then come home to his garden and his family. He envisioned a contented wife who would enjoy taking care of the children, cleaning the house, and cooking fine dinners. Essie Brown had other ideas. She ignored housework, prepared hasty meals, and spent most of her household allowance on acting lessons. She was a forceful, determined woman; he was a quiet, peace-loving man. He let her do as she liked.

By the time Helen arrived, Essie Brown had joined a touring theater company. Because Frank Brown was often away from home on business trips, Helen's mother sent the little girl to live with her own mother, now a widow. Meanwhile, Essie Brown traveled from town to town, appearing in a show called *Liberty Belles*.

Helen loved to listen to her "graddy" tell ghost stories and tales of her childhood, to watch her work on her ever-present embroidery, to see her taking one of her celebrated coconut cakes from the oven. "Everything about Graddy Hayes was warm and safe and loving," Helen Hayes noted years afterward. "She was the last of the generation of real grandmothers."

Weekends, when Frank Brown usually managed to get home, became high points in his daughter's life. "Father took the world as he found it and

The Washington Senators line up in 1918. Helen observed that at the ballpark, her usually soft-spoken father turned into a normal, screaming baseball fan.

relished what was within his reach," recalled his daughter. The two particularly enjoyed listening to the U.S. Marine Band at the Washington Monument, riding on the Ferris wheel at a nearby amusement park, and sitting in the bleachers to watch the Washington Senators. At the ballpark, quiet, mild-mannered Frank Brown became another man, shouting encouragement to his team and screaming at the umpires. "This was his ball field and it was a world which he understood," recalled his daughter. "He knew whom he was for and whom he was against. And he let them know it. When we went home, he was himself again. The gentlest, kindest, dearest man who ever lived."

Helen loved her grandmother and her father, but she adored her mother. Every few weeks, Essie Brown would sweep back into her daughter's world, filling the house with laughter and enchanting the little girl with tales of theatrical glitter and excitement. When she was home, nothing could induce Helen to leave her side. But her mother's visits provided Helen with anxiety as well as gaiety: Essie Brown's riotous stories about touring in *Liberty Belles* masked the distinctly unglamorous reality of life on the road.

Brown spent her days traveling from one seedy theater to another, presenting a second-rate production to sparse, sometimes rowdy audiences. She liked the applause but not the grimy dressing rooms and dreary hotels she shared with her colleagues. When the troupe's management found itself short of funds, the actors received no pay. More

Frank Brown relaxes with his dog, Beau, in the backyard of his Washington, D.C., home. Unlike his glamour-seeking wife, Helen's father cherished the quiet life.

than once, an unhappy Essie Brown had been forced to sneak out of a hotel at dawn to avoid paying for her room.

Full of high spirits one minute, Essie Brown could be morose or angry the next. She bitterly resented the drabness of her marriage, the burdens of motherhood, and the lack of glamour in her life. Without warning, she might turn on her daughter, berating the bewildered little girl for some imagined offense or childish mistake. When he was at home, Frank Brown also felt the lash of his wife's pent-up rage and frustration. Both father and child, however, submitted to these scenes without protest. Frank Brown loved peace; Helen

21

Brown loved her mother. Wanting her approval more than anything else, Helen tried hard to please her. At an early age, she learned that playacting was the best way to do it.

One day, after her mother had staged a particularly unpleasant scene, five-year-old Helen made an announcement: She was running away forever, and she needed five cents for the streetcar. Diverted by the game, Essie Brown gave Helen the nickel and held the door open. When half an hour passed and Helen had not returned, her mother went to look for her. She found her on a nearby park bench, still clutching her nickel. Even as a mature woman, Helen Hayes would never forget that happy moment, when her mother proved she loved her by going out to find her. Helen held out her hand. "Buy whatever you want with my five cents," she said.

On another occasion, Helen raised her mother's spirits by imitating *Cleopatra in Her Barge*, a painting the two had seen at a local museum. Back home, Essie Hayes discovered her naked daughter in the tub, holding a fan and wearing a towel wrapped around her head. "And who do you think *you* are?" she asked. "I'm Clee O'Patrick in her bath!" responded Helen loftily. Essie Brown broke into peals of delighted laughter.

Helen's efforts not only amused her mother but made her believe the child had dramatic talent. In her memoirs, Essie Brown recalled that she now began to realize her daughter had the "God-given gift" she lacked herself.

From this point on, she would concentrate on making her daughter a star. "With Catherine Hayes [the Swan of Erin] lurking in my past and Mother now seeing to my future," wrote Helen Hayes later, "my destiny seemed assured."

Essie and Helen Brown began to go to every stage performance available. They were always first in line to buy 25-cent tickets for the "rush-seats," so called because their purchasers rushed for the balcony the instant the theater doors opened. While her mother climbed the four long flights of stairs as quickly as she could, small, agile Helen scampered ahead, darting between the legs of irate adults and pouncing on front-row seats in the balcony.

"Excruciatingly shy, I would clutch the two seats with whitening knuckles and stiffening toes, my lips a thin determined line, my eyes tight shut to avoid the sharp glances of the outraged losers," Hayes recalled in her 1968 autobiography. When her mother reached the balcony, she would catch her breath and start reading the program to her daughter. The two relished everything they saw, from Shakespeare's tragedy *Hamlet* to Franz Lehár's operetta *The Merry Widow*.

Helen's education, of course, could not be limited to museums and theaters. But when the time came for her to start school, her mother hesitated. The law required all public-school children to receive smallpox vaccinations, but Essie Brown (mistakenly) considered such inoculations dangerous. She decided to send Helen to a private

After Helen made her first Broadway appearance, at Lew Fields's Herald Square Theatre (above) in 1909, Essie Brown changed her daughter's name from Brown to Hayes.

school where vaccinations were not required. Accordingly, she enrolled Helen in the local Roman Catholic institution, Holy Cross Academy. It was at Holy Cross that five-year-old Helen made her theatrical debut, playing Peaseblossom, one of the fairies in Shakespeare's comedy *A Midsummer Night's Dream*.

When Helen was seven years old, her mother sent her to dancing class. The following year, the school held its annual afternoon recital at Washington's Belasco Theatre. Allowed to borrow

scenery from the professional company then performing at the Belasco, the school invited the company's star, Lew Fields, to its show. One half of Weber and Fields, the nation's most celebrated comedy team, Fields was also a powerful Broadway producer and the owner of two New York City theaters. To everyone's surprise, he came to watch the dance recital.

For her part in the show, Helen sang "Gibson Girl Bathing Beauty," a sultry but funny song from a current Broadway musical. Obviously impressed

Always small for her age, eight-year-old Helen plays five-year-old Claudia in The Prince Chap, *staged by the Columbia Players of Washington, D.C., in early 1909.*

with the tiny, vibrant performer, Lew Fields wrote a note to the Belasco's manager after the show. If the Browns wanted a Broadway career for their daughter, he said, he would be happy to help. Essie Brown reacted to Fields's letter with delight, but her husband felt differently. For once putting his foot down, Frank Brown said a trip to New York was out of the question. Helen could perform on stage, he said, but she was to live at home and go to school.

In May 1909, four months after Helen's appearance at the Belasco, Fred Burger called on her mother. Burger, who had produced *Liberty Belles*, was now running a Washington theater group called the Columbia Players, and he needed a child actress for his upcoming production of *The Prince Chap*. Helen, he said, would be ideal for the play, which also had a small role suitable for her mother. "And so," recalled Helen Hayes later, "I made my debut with Mother." Impressed with Helen's work over the summer, the Columbia Players' director told Essie Hayes that her daughter's talent was being wasted. She should, he said, be in New York City, the nation's theatrical capital. Essie Brown needed no further encouragement. Somehow persuading her husband to part with $50—a week's salary—she bought two train tickets and headed north with her daughter.

"How incredible it now seems," wrote Helen Hayes decades after that first visit to Manhattan, "the naïve, brisk little woman and the skinny, innocent child, essaying to storm, without equipment, preparation, or knowl- edge, the established battlements of the commercial theater." But storm it they did. Fields kept them waiting outside his office door for hours. When he finally appeared, Essie Brown waved a photograph of Helen, costumed as the Gibson Girl, in his face. "You do remember Helen, don't you, Mr. Fields?" she demanded.

Lew Fields indeed remembered the nine-year-old performer. Before the afternoon was over, Essie Brown had signed her daughter to a contract for Fields's next play, a Victor Herbert operetta called *Old Dutch*. Helen's salary was to be $35 per week—"almost as much as your father earns!" exulted mother to daughter. Frank Brown had lost his daughter to the stage. As it turned out, he also lost his share in her name. "Hayes," advised knowledgeable New Yorkers, would look better on a theater marquee than plain old "Brown."

As the Little Mime in *Old Dutch*, Helen stood to one side of the stage, imitating the leading lady's gestures and mouthing the words as she sang. "My pantomime was a humorous comment on the singer's style," noted Hayes later. Her performance brought down the house. The day after *Old Dutch* opened, on November 22, 1909, Broadway had a new star: Helen Hayes. "In this clever tot, Mr. Fields has the greatest leading woman of her size," wrote the New York *Evening World*'s drama critic. "She tumbles the house into laughter," he continued. "The longing in her dreamy eyes and the yearning in her outstretched arms make her seem more than seven [Helen's age, according to Fields's publicity staff]. The kiddie knows a thing or two."

Indeed, Helen seemed a born professional. From the beginning, she memorized her lines, her cues, and her bits of stage business flawlessly. Before each of the 88 performances of *Old Dutch*, Helen painstakingly applied her own makeup. Her dedication to this process intrigued the other company

As the Little Mime in Lew Fields's musical Old Dutch, *Helen earned her first rave reviews. One first-nighter called her "the greatest leading woman of her size."*

members, who often gathered at her dressing room door to watch, half-impressed and half-amused. Always a rather solitary child, Helen had made few friends of her own age as a little girl. But she was comfortable with adults, and she soon became the pet of Lew Fields and the rest of the show's staff.

In 1910, after the successful run of *Old Dutch*, Fields signed Helen to a comedy called *The Summer Widowers*. Helen played Psyche Finnegan, a character she later described as "an early-day Lucy from *Peanuts*." Audiences and critics applauded the tiny comedian, especially for her "tart scene." In this routine, a midget dressed as a little boy showed Psyche-Helen a delicious-looking raspberry tart. "That's not raspberry. Anybody can see it's strawberry," she said. She took a bite, decided it might be blackberry, then took another bite to be sure. After devouring the whole pastry, she casually dusted her hands on the midget's sleeve, then strolled off the stage as her costar complained, "You can't never trust a woman." Theatergoers howled.

On days when she had no afternoon performance, Helen attended classes at a Manhattan Catholic school; on other days, her mother tutored her. School authorities of the time were far more relaxed about enforcing attendance than they are today. Although Helen's on-and-off schooling and her show business way of life were unlike those of most young people, they were perfectly legal. They left her father, however, both puzzled and dismayed: "He didn't have the foggiest notion of what the theater was all about," recalled his daughter later.

But Frank Brown trusted his wife to look after Helen's best interests, and he looked forward to the occasional Sundays when "his girls" managed to come home for a visit. "Father seemed always to be waving goodbye at the railroad station, getting smaller and smaller in my life, his brave smile blurring more and more as we chugged away," his daughter would sadly recall. One of her visits home left the little girl heartbroken: She and her mother returned for the funeral of her grandmother, who died suddenly in 1910. "The finality of death was beyond me," wrote Helen Hayes later. "I just couldn't believe that my Graddy was gone."

When Helen and her mother returned to New York, they ran into their old friend Frederick Thompson, former director of the Columbia Players. Now directing silent one-reelers for the pioneering Vitagraph Studio, Thompson invited Helen to star in one of his films. Although most theater people considered the new medium far be-

Hayes (left foreground) plays a shy young woman in the 1917 film The Weavers of Life, *one of several silent movies the actress made between 1910 and 1917.*

Manhattan's Empire Theatre attracted patrons with just two words: John Drew. The popular actor found 14-year-old Helen so charming that he allowed her to share his curtain calls.

neath them, Essie Brown felt indebted to Thompson, and she allowed Helen to appear in *Jean and the Calico Doll*, a melodrama in which Jean (played by Helen) falls into a ravine and is rescued by her faithful collie.

The young actress thoroughly enjoyed her first movie, which involved a trip to the New Jersey countryside in a long row of automobiles. When the director spotted a setting he liked—which happened to be a private estate—he simply unloaded his crew and filmed the scene. Shooting ended when the estate's owner chased the moviemakers off the property. Hayes later reported that she had "much more fun" making that movie than she had in Hollywood 25 years afterward. "All the spontaneity was gone by then," she said. "Everyone was important, and innocence was lost." As for the quality of her acting in her first film, she said that a friend "later told me I was better than the collie."

Twelve years old in 1912, Helen found herself out of work. Having reached what she called "the awkward age"—too old to play young children and too young for adult roles—she returned home with her mother. Assuming that his wife and daughter were back for good, the delighted Frank Brown bought a new house in Washington. Helen was, she wrote later, "cozy and content to be home with Father," but Essie Brown was anything but content. Two years of New York's glamorous theatrical world had made the life of a housewife seem duller than ever.

"Mother was again a seething captive," recalled her daughter.

Essie Brown tried to do what was expected of her. Imitating her neighbors, she cooked, cleaned, put up preserves, and collected recipes, but, noted Helen, she hated "every solitary minute of it." Her old depressions and mood swings returned and, even more damaging to her husband and daughter, she began to drink heavily. "Our little house came tumbling down as Mother alternated between light-headed evenings and guilt-ridden daily retreats," Hayes recalled. Night after night, Helen lay awake in her room, listening to her father help his staggering wife up the stairs. Afraid and ashamed, Helen buried her face in the pillow and cried.

One day Helen came home from school and found her father in tears. "There wasn't the slightest doubt who had put them there," she wrote later. For Helen, this was the last straw. She ran down the hall, found her mother fixing a drink, and seized her by the arms. "I actually shook my mother," she recalled. "Go inside and say you're sorry, do you hear?" she screamed. "Say you're sorry to my father!" Mother and daughter faced each other for a long, silent moment. Then Essie Brown slowly followed Helen's orders. From that moment on, Helen and her mother reversed their roles. Barely a teenager herself, Helen took over the job of homemaker, cleaning the house, preparing the family meals, and keeping an eye on her mother.

A stroke of good luck ended Helen's unhappy situation: When she was 14, a telegram arrived from New York City. Signed by Broadway producer Charles Frohman, the wire asked Essie Brown to bring her daughter to read for a part in *The Prodigal Husband*, a new play starring the celebrated John Drew. The prospect of returning to Broadway had an almost miraculous effect on Essie Brown. "Mother saw a light at the end of the tunnel and she regained her balance immediately," recalled her daughter. Once again, the two boarded a train and headed north.

Greeting Helen and her mother at the Empire Theatre was coproducer Alfred Hayman, a gruff, loud-voiced man known for his dislike of "kiddie" stars. "Can you act?" he barked at Helen. She curtsied demurely, looked him in the eye, and said, "Yes." Impressing the director, the producer, and the star with her reading, Helen got the part. *The Prodigal Husband*, she said later, was "a sleazy romantic comedy," but John Drew's name on the marquee attracted the cream of New York's high society. When Helen peeked out from backstage on opening night, she recalled, she saw a glittering crowd, "dressed to the teeth in their fine feathers, pearls, furs, and blinding diamonds. Long, white-gloved arms politely waved to each other until the whole orchestra looked like a sea of swans."

After eight weeks in New York, *The Prodigal Husband* made a tour of the eastern seaboard. Traveling from town to town by railroad, the young actress and her mother often slept in drafty rooms above saloons or next to train stations. But the troupe played to packed houses, and Helen basked in the admiration of the great John Drew. He took his young costar sight-seeing at every stop, coached her in French, and insisted on sharing his curtain calls with her. "A tour with John Drew," noted Hayes later, "was filled with bouquets of violets and no plumbing." After five months on the road, the tour ended, and Helen went back to school at the Sacred Heart Convent in Washington.

For the next two years, Helen attended classes and appeared in local theatrical productions. When she was almost 17, a New York talent scout saw her playing a 10-year-old girl in a comedy called *The Dummy* and asked her to audition for producer George C. Tyler. Once again traveling to New York with her mother, Helen Hayes tried out for the road-company lead in *Pollyanna* and got the job. Suffocatingly sentimental, *Pollyanna* revolved around the "glad girl," a brave and eternally cheerful young woman who finds goodness in everything and everybody. In one of the play's typical scenes, for example, Pollyanna is carried onstage after breaking both her legs in an accident. "I'm so glad, glad, *glad* it happened! For you have to lose your legs to really love them!" she shouts happily.

Despite her character's numbing sweetness, Hayes managed to make her portrayal genuinely moving. One night in Montana, she feared she would be laughed—or even booed—off the stage

Seventeen years old but still childlike in appearance, Hayes sits for a portrait during the 1917 tour of her saccharine but hugely successful play, Pollyanna.

Hayes and her mother relax between Pollyanna *performances. Determined to make Hayes a star, Essie Brown managed every detail of her daughter's early career.*

by the audience of tough-looking cow-hands. Indeed, after her "glad" broken-leg scene, she heard suspicious hissing sounds from the orchestra seats. But when she peeked out after the curtain fell, she saw that most of the leathery cowpokes were blowing their noses, trying to hide their tears. Reviewing Hayes as Pollyanna, critics found themselves using such words as *restrained*, *poised*, and *sincere*.

When Hayes spoke publicly about her *Pollyanna* role, she kept in character. "I have always been of a happy nature, but not until I began to play the Glad Girl did I realize how helpful the happy-natured may be by exerting their influence on others," she said at one point. Privately, however, her attitude was more down-to-earth. She told friends that if she ever heard the word *glad* again, she would scream.

Hayes listens raptly as William Gillette, her Dear Brutus *costar, offers professional advice. Watching Gillette work, said Hayes, "was equal to a full dramatic course."*

THREE

"One Long Search
for Truth"

When *Pollyanna* closed in mid-1918, Hayes had no trouble finding a job. Impressed by the young actress's work, producer George Tyler had decided to take her under his professional wing: He had a new play ready and waiting for her. Hayes was delighted to acquire a manager whose other clients had included such theatrical superstars as Sarah Bernhardt and Eleonora Duse. "On plain faith, with no written contract," she wrote later, "Mr. Tyler took over my career."

The new play was *Penrod*, a comedy based on Booth Tarkington's popular 1914 novel. Although Hayes received good notices for her portrayal of the hero's sister—her first adult role—the play failed to excite critics and closed quickly. Even before its final curtain, however, Hayes had received another, more exciting offer: Producer Alf Hayman wanted her to play Margaret in *Dear Brutus*, a drama by one of the

era's finest playwrights, Sir James M. Barrie.

Because Hayes was now under Tyler's management, she needed his approval to take Hayman's offer. To her alarm, Tyler told Hayman that his client was available for the role, but only at a salary of $300 per week—twice the amount she had received for *Penrod*, by far her highest-paid role. Hayman, who badly wanted Hayes for the role of Margaret, agreed to Tyler's demand, and Hayes took on her most successful role to date. She loved playing Margaret, "a regular girl," especially after Pollyanna. "It's such a relief not to have to be glad any more!" she said.

Costarring with Hayes in *Dear Brutus* was William Gillette, an immensely popular stage actor who had made a career out of playing Sherlock Holmes. Assuring Hayes that she could become a great actress, Gillette as-

The Scottish dramatist Sir James M. Barrie, author of Hayes's 1918 hit, Dear Brutus, *is best remembered for his popular* Peter Pan, *written in 1904.*

signed himself to teach her everything he could. His first move was to help her polish her accent. The rest of the cast, the American-born Gillette included, spoke with crisp British accents; next to them, Hayes's natural Maryland drawl sounded out of place. To correct her speech, Gillette gave her a copy of

Shakespeare's sonnets and instructed her to read them aloud until her intonation improved. That problem overcome, Gillette set to work on Hayes's performance, which he considered badly shaped by the play's director. Coaching Hayes in secret, Gillette told her to follow the director's instructions during rehearsals but to play her scenes his way on opening night.

When the play began its out-of-town run in Atlantic City, New Jersey, it was a disaster. Trying to combine the director's view of her character, Gillette's interpretation, and her own ideas, Hayes delivered a confused, unsatisfying performance. "I felt no truth in anything I had done," she said mournfully. "I didn't believe in my Margaret." After listening to the director's scathing criticism following the first performance, Hayes fled the theater, walking for miles as she discussed her mistakes with her mother. When she finally returned to her hotel, she found "the wonderful and patient Mr. Gillette" awaiting her.

"Alf Hayman said to tell you that he is prouder than ever of his little leading lady," said Gillette, "and by the way, my dear, so am I." Hayes was still disgusted with her performance, but the expression of faith from the two men gave her hope. By the time the show opened in Washington, Hayes felt much more confident about her work; her proud father, who saw the play there, naturally thought it was wonderful.

Dear Brutus opened in New York just before Christmas, 1918. The night, recalled Hayes afterward, "was everything Mr. Gillette promised." When the third-act curtain fell, she said, "we stood up to a formidable crashing roar, a Niagara Falls of sound. I had never before heard anything like it." Grabbing Hayes's hand, Gillette took a curtain call, then another. Still, the crowd roared. Hayes tried to wrench her hand free. The audience, she thought, was applauding the great William Gillette; who was she to share in his glory? But Gillette refused to release her hand until they had taken 20 bows. Then the towering actor looked down on his tiny costar. "You didn't think I was going to take those curtain calls alone, did you?" he asked. "Those curtains were for you."

The next day, New York's drama critics outdid themselves in praising the young actress. According to Heywood Broun of the *Herald Tribune*, "Miss Helen Hayes is as eager as a Christmas morning and as dazzling as a Christmas night." Dorothy Parker, a writer renowned for her savage wit and cynicism, said Hayes had done "an exquisite piece of acting. . . . *Dear Brutus* made me weep—and I can't possibly enjoy a play more than that." At the age of 18, Helen Hayes was a Broadway star.

Hayes gave Gillette generous credit for her success. "His intelligence and control were remarkable," she noted. "Just being on the same stage with him for one evening was equal to a full dramatic course." Other valued advisers included an actress who had told Hayes how to make audiences respond to Pollyanna. "You must learn to play the part without crying," she said. "If *you* cry, honey, *they* don't!" And Hayes always remembered the elderly performer who once told her how to deal with stage fright. "When you feel nervous and you want to tense something," said the old actress, "curl your

When producer George Tyler took Hayes under his wing, he earned the resentment of Essie Brown. A classic "stage mother," she wanted sole authority over her actress daughter.

toes, Dearie. They're inside your shoes and nobody will see what you're doing." "I spent years curling my toes and was forever grateful," Hayes remarked in her 1968 autobiography.

Manager George Tyler, too, proved an invaluable counselor. "Everything he did was for my good," Hayes wrote later, "if not my joy." Gruff, sometimes dictatorial, Tyler took complete charge of Hayes's professional life, buying production rights for plays he thought would suit her and sometimes commissioning plays especially for her. He even told the 18 year old what books

she should read to improve her mind.

Working under Tyler's management, however, presented certain problems. Although he spared no expense in theater productions, Tyler did not pay his actors very well. More awkward for Hayes, he adamantly opposed her joining Actors' Equity, the theatrical labor union. Most of Hayes's friends belonged to Equity, and they urged the young actress to demonstrate her solidarity by joining them. Although she "felt like a traitor," she recalled years later, she feared invoking the anger of her fierce manager. "My chums weren't angry," she said, "but they were all disappointed that I wouldn't stand up to Mr. Tyler. But I hadn't been encouraged to stand up to anyone in my life."

Following Tyler's dictates did provide Hayes with some choice roles. In 1920, he commissioned *Bab*, a light comedy based on Mary Roberts Rinehart's popular "subdeb" stories. When *Bab* opened in Boston, it made Hayes the woman of the hour, especially among Harvard students. Lines of young men formed at the stage door after each performance, waiting to see the giddy debutante they had adored onstage. Hayes's dressing room soon overflowed with elaborate bouquets, giant boxes of candy, and invitations to dances and late suppers. Students by the dozens cut classes and failed tests in order to see *Bab* again and again. "Babism had taken over Harvard," recalled Hayes happily. "It was divine."

Although Hayes basked in what she called "my first burst of personal pop-

ularity," her mother frowned on it. Essie Brown had not worked this long and this hard to see her daughter's career thrown away on some frivolous romance—or marriage. Brown opened every invitation, accepting only those she considered "innocuous," and she chaperoned every date she accepted for her daughter.

When one young man, carried away by the charms of "Bab," asked Helen Hayes to marry him, her mother firmly stepped in, visiting the suitor's aunt and informing her that Hayes had no intention of marrying anyone. Although she later admitted resenting her mother's "interference and her power," Hayes never rebelled. "[Mother] was utterly committed and dedicated to my future," she recalled. "Without her, I might have laughed, tossed my head, and danced my way right off the stage."

A smash hit in Boston, *Bab* crashed in New York. Tense about seeing her name in lights five stories high—HELEN HAYES IN BAB, read the marquee—Hayes gave a high-pitched, nervous performance on opening night. Critics sneered. Even Heywood Broun, who had once compared Hayes to Christmas morning, dismissed her portrayal of Bab with one stinging word: *cute*. His review, said Hayes, left her "shattered

Hayes strikes a demure pose as Bab, the "subdeb" character created by novelist Mary Roberts Rinehart. Wildly popular in Boston, Bab *received disastrous notices in New York City.*

Actress Minnie Maddern Fiske, 55 years old when Hayes saw her in 1920, filled the young performer with awe. Fiske's work, said Hayes, "was never one jot less than perfect."

because I felt he was right, furious because he *was* right." She realized it was time to take a long look at her own work.

Hayes knew her voice sometimes sounded shrill, that she spoke too slowly at times, that her performances varied in quality from one night to the next. Was it possible that after spending most of her life on the stage, she did not really know much about acting? She asked her friend Ruth Chatterton for advice. The veteran actress minced no words. "Okay, Helen, I've always thought you had talent," she said. But then, holding her thumb and forefinger a fraction of an inch apart, she added, "You don't have *that* much technique."

On Chatterton's advice, Hayes began taking lessons from Frances Robinson Duff, a highly respected drama coach. Duff taught her how to control her breathing, how to use her voice more effectively, how to express her emotions through body movements, how to ration her energy. "I improved immediately," recalled Hayes. "Talent may not be for sale, but the best way to package and display your gift is." Eventually, she said, "I learned that the actor's life is just one long search for the ability to be absolutely truthful."

Hayes now began to study the work of the best actors working in New York. Watching one of her favorites, Minnie Maddern Fiske, she realized that however spontaneous Fiske appeared, each of her performances was precisely calculated, from the lightest sigh to the most casual gesture.

Hayes's stagecraft had consisted almost entirely of her own instincts. Now she understood that in order to give a first-rate performance time after time, she had to know exactly how and why she made each vocal change and each movement.

Perhaps responding to Hayes's desire for self-improvement, Tyler announced that she must go to Paris and study European culture. He made the first-class ship and hotel reservations; Hayes had to pay for them. Her mother protested the extravagance of the trip, but Tyler said Hayes was now a star and must live like one. "The public expects you to live on a grand scale," he told Hayes. Obedient as always, Hayes made the trip, although she and her mother secretly exchanged the expensive reservations for the cheapest available.

Meeting Hayes and Brown in France, Tyler led them on a whirlwind tour. They rode through the countryside in his chauffeur-driven car, speeding past castles, cathedrals, and scenic lanes where Hayes would have liked to linger. In Paris, they marched double-time through historic streets and museums. In Tyler's "introduction to Gallic history," noted Hayes wryly, "the French Revolution seemed to have lasted ten minutes." After two frantic weeks, Tyler left for London, instructing Hayes and her mother to join him there the next day. Instead, for the first time, Hayes defied her mentor, staying on in Paris with her mother to enjoy the city at their own pace. "I was sure that Mr. Tyler would kill me," she recalled.

Traffic swirls around the Paris Opera in the 1920s. When Hayes visited the French capital in 1920, her manager, George Tyler, gave her little time to admire the city's sights.

As it turned out, the producer had no time to scold Hayes for her independent attitude. He had lined up three plays for her, and he put her to work the moment she returned to New York. The first play, *The Wren*, had been written especially for Hayes by Booth Tarkington. Although he had modeled the central character on her, the young actress detested the part. "I play a very bossy young person who can't help managing and mothering all the people around her," Hayes told a friend. "I'm not that way a bit in real life." The play, which opened on Hayes's 21st birthday—October 10, 1921—proved as unpopular with patrons as it was with its star; it closed after 24 performances. Tyler's next vehicle, *Golden Days*, proved equally disappointing at the box office, surviving for only 40 performances.

The third play was another story. Entitled *To the Ladies*, it was the work of the celebrated playwrights Marc Connelly and George S. Kaufman, co-authors of one of the year's biggest Broadway hits, *Merton of the Movies*. Before rehearsals for *To the Ladies* began, the playwrights visited Hayes to discuss the project. Kaufman mentioned that Hayes's character was musical. "Do you play the piano?" he

Stage star Marie Dressler (in long white dress) leads a protest during the Actors' Equity strike of 1919. Defying her manager, Hayes joined the theater union in 1924.

asked. "Of course," said Hayes, who had never played a note in her life. Two flops in a row had left her almost broke, but as soon as Connelly and Kaufman left, she and her mother rushed out to buy a $750 piano on credit. When rehearsals began six weeks later, she could sing and play the script's songs with ease. The play opened to rave reviews in February 1922, allowing Hayes to draw a relieved breath; now, she thought, she could pay for that piano.

To the Ladies enjoyed a long Broadway run and a successful national tour. Not long afterward, Hayes had lunch with a fellow actor who asked why she had still not joined Actors' Equity. "You belong with your family, Helen—the other kids who are struggling," he said. Hayes said she wanted to join, but that Tyler would not allow it. Tired of Hayes's dogged loyalty to the domineering Tyler, her friend revealed what was common knowledge on Broadway: Tyler had been regularly refusing offers for Hayes without even telling her. When the wildly successful songwriter-star George M. Cohan had asked for Hayes to star in his recent smash hit, *In Love With Love*, for example, Tyler had given the part to another actress and signed Hayes for a sad little British comedy that ran for less than three weeks.

For Hayes, who had been increasingly unhappy about Tyler's tyrannical ways, this was the last straw. She decided to join the union. Working up her courage, she went to Tyler's office and told him of her decision. As she had

known he would, Tyler reacted with fury. "If you walk out of this office," he thundered, "there is no turning back!" Hayes walked out.

She was relieved to be free of Tyler's control, but she bore him no ill will. Many years later, in fact, she helped support her former mentor when his career collapsed. "Before he dismissed me, he had made me one of the leading young stars in New York," she wrote later. "It was a painful sensation, but George C. Tyler had done such a good job that my career could now soar without him."

Charles Gordon MacArthur swept Hayes off her feet with his first remark to her. Pouring peanuts into her hand, he said, "I wish they were emeralds."

FOUR

"The Catch of All Time"

A few months after Hayes left George Tyler's management, producer Edgar Selwyn asked her to take the lead in his upcoming musical, *Dancing Mothers*. Her part would be that of yet another dizzy young woman, a character she was thoroughly tired of portraying. Yearning to play Juliet or Cleopatra, she wanted to decline *Dancing Mothers*, but she did not want to offend Selwyn. To get her out of the situation gracefully, Essie Brown—now acting as Hayes's agent—told Selwyn that her daughter would work for no less than $750 per week. When he agreed to the sky-high wage, Hayes was trapped. She opened in the show in August 1924.

Received with critical cheers, *Dancing Mothers* would run for almost a year, confirming Hayes's status as a leading woman on Broadway. Offstage, however, she still felt like a child. No one shared her life but Essie Brown, who filled the roles of mother, room-mate, confidante, traveling companion, and manager. At the age of 24, Hayes's social life had been limited to her Boston fling as Bab; her only romance had been with the stage. Forever in the company of her strong-willed mother, Hayes felt shy and ill at ease around young people, especially young male people.

But all this changed one afternoon in 1924. That November day, she ran into playwright Marc Connelly, who asked her to go to a party with him. Knowing that half the celebrities in New York would be there, the shy Hayes dragged her feet, but Connelly insisted, and she finally agreed. The party was in full swing when they arrived. Among those trading witty barbs and roaring at one another's jokes were comedian Harpo Marx, songwriter Irving Berlin, composer George Gershwin, and columnists Alexander Woollcott, Robert Benchley, and Dorothy Parker.

Dorothy Parker works on a manuscript in the 1920s. A leading member of Manhattan's literary set—and a former girlfriend of Charles MacArthur—Parker heaped scorn on Hayes.

Although Hayes had met most of these people, she had never felt comfortable with them. "Their gossip," she recalled, "was way over my head," and she was sure they considered her "a simpleton or stone-deaf or possibly both." She was not far wrong. New York's glitterati, as this throng was sometimes labeled, regarded Hayes as a sweet but colorless waif. Helen, remarked humorist Robert Benchley, "makes Pollyanna seem like a painted hussy."

Overwhelmed by this roomful of chattering, cocktail-sipping sophisticates, Hayes retreated to a secluded corner. As Irving Berlin played his popular song "Always" on the piano, Hayes wondered what she could say if anybody came to talk to her. Then a handsome man appeared at her side. "Wanna peanut?" he asked. As Hayes described him later, this "enchanting creature" had green-flecked hazel eyes, curly hair, pointed ears, and a mouth "designed exclusively for smiling." She accepted a peanut; he poured her a handful from a crumpled paper bag.

"I wish they were emeralds," said Charles MacArthur.

MacArthur spent the rest of the party at Hayes's side, took her home in a horse-drawn cab, and promised to call her. "I didn't believe my luck," Hayes wrote years later. "The catch of all time had singled me out. . . . It was just too good to be true." And in the beginning, it was. MacArthur did not call. Days passed, then weeks. Hayes talked about MacArthur constantly; why, she kept asking her mother, didn't he call? It was just as well that he didn't, asserted Essie Brown. Helen's work, she said, was too important to be interrupted by any man. But Hayes could not get that "beautiful man" off her mind. "I was smitten mightily," she wrote later.

When the phone did ring one day, Essie Brown answered. The caller was not MacArthur but Theresa Helburn of the Theatre Guild, offering Hayes her dream role: the female lead in George

Hayes and MacArthur hold hands in 1928. "What on earth are they doing together?" asked one friend. "Charlie's a man of the world and she makes Pollyanna seem like a painted hussy."

Bernard Shaw's *Caesar and Cleopatra*. With its limited budget, said Helburn, the guild could pay only $250 per week. Essie Hayes hung up without a word. When Hayes realized what her mother had done, she raced out to a corner phone booth, called Helburn, and accepted her offer. "Nobody was going to stop me from playing Cleopatra," she wrote later. "It was difficult to cross mother, but I *had* to play that part."

Caesar and Cleopatra failed to please the critics, but its run brought Hayes something better than good reviews. Every night before the curtain rose, she peeked out at the audience, hoping MacArthur would be in it. He never was. Then, without warning, he suddenly appeared backstage. He had been walking past the theater, he said, and noticed Hayes's picture out front. Would she have supper with him after the performance?

"I can't," she said miserably. She and her mother were staying at a friend's house on Long Island, and she was expected that night. Then an idea struck her. It was a bold thought, but she had to do something or she might never see MacArthur again. She invited him to come and spend the weekend with her and her mother. To her astonishment, he accepted.

Giddily, Hayes called her mother to announce MacArthur's impending arrival. His visit, she knew, would not be met with approval. A romance for her daughter did not suit Essie Brown; she had been secretly delighted by MacArthur's failure to call. "So that tramp is the one you've been raving about,"

she said after she met him. "She had thought Charlie was out of the picture," Hayes wrote later. "But after that weekend, he was never to be out of it again."

Five years older than Hayes, Charles MacArthur had grown up with his seven brothers and sisters in Nyack, a small town north of New York City. The children's father, William Telfer MacArthur, was a fiery fundamentalist preacher who could, according to Hayes, "smell a sinner five miles away on a windless day." A strict disciplinarian, the senior MacArthur often punished his children's "wickedness" by whipping them with a vinegar-soaked leather strap.

Charles MacArthur was educated at Wilson Academy, a missionary training school whose rules were almost as strict as Reverend MacArthur's: Students were forbidden to dance, watch movies, read unapproved books, or associate with the "godless" local high school students. As soon as he graduated, MacArthur fled this rigid and sanctimonious world. In 1916 he joined a U.S. military expedition hunting bandit-rebel Pancho Villa in Mexico; when America entered World War I in 1917, he signed up immediately and soon saw action on the battlefields of France.

After the war, MacArthur took a job with the Chicago *Examiner* and, at the age of 22, married a fellow reporter. The young couple soon separated, but because neither planned to marry anyone else, they took no steps toward divorce. MacArthur moved to New

Noticing Hayes's picture outside New York City's Guild Theatre (above), Charles MacArthur went backstage to invite the young star to dinner.

York, where he quickly landed a job at the *American Weekly* newspaper, began to write plays, and became the new star of Manhattan's social and literary worlds.

Charlie MacArthur may have been the most popular man in New York. Witty, unpredictable, generous, and irreverent, he exuded a magnetism that attracted close male friends and even closer woman friends. As Hayes put it later, "To men of all stations, he was a pal and tireless drinking companion. To women, he was a goal often achieved." Novelist F. Scott Fitzgerald characterized MacArthur in two sentences: "Other men have to *do*. Charlie only has to *be*."

After MacArthur's weekend with Hayes and her mother, the actress and the journalist became inseparable. Everywhere MacArthur went, from cocktail parties to country picnics to evenings at the theater, Hayes went too. Although the unsophisticated, rather prim Hayes and the devil-may-care Charlie MacArthur were worlds apart in background and philosophy, they found themselves deeply in love.

MacArthur's cronies put up with Hayes as long as she was only "Charlie's girl," but when they realized he planned to marry her, they were horrified. Hayes described their feelings: "Charlie was going to be taken out of circulation, and that awful little Helen was responsible." Actress Ethel Barrymore, a close friend of MacArthur's, said of Hayes, "She's a monster!" Another actress, glamorous Tallulah Bankhead, expressed shock at the MacArthur-Hayes pairing. "Charlie MacArthur is a well-known skirt-chaser," she said. "I surely thought naïve little Helen was saving herself for the boy next door."

Associates were also concerned for Hayes's sake. Theater critic Alexander Woollcott, a good friend of both Hayes and MacArthur, took her to lunch and said gently, "Can you live on the razor's edge, Helen? Do you really think you can hang chintz curtains on the lip of Vesuvius and call it home?" Hayes thought for a moment, then replied, "I know I can't give Charlie excitement, but he has enough for everybody. What I can give him—or die trying—is contentment and some degree of peace."

Hayes's response may have calmed Woollcott, but nothing, it seemed, could calm Essie Brown. "You're making a fatal mistake," she warned her daughter. "I love him, Mother," responded Hayes. *"Love!"* sneered Brown. "What about your career? The first thing you know, you'll have children. What then?" Hayes said she and MacArthur planned to wait. "Wait? Ha!" her mother said bitterly. "That's what I said when I married Frank Brown—and look what happened to me!" Both women suddenly fell silent. Hayes was hurt but not deterred. "At no time," she wrote later, "did I consider any alternative to marrying Charlie."

Hayes meant what she said. Nobody was going to stop her: not mother, not friends, not MacArthur's evangelist father, who roared, "You are a sinner! No son of mine will ever marry an ac-

Writer Alexander Woollcott oversees production of one of his books. Fond of both Hayes and MacArthur, Woollcott served as best man at their 1928 wedding.

tress!'' Not even the Roman Catholic church, which would excommunicate her for marrying a divorced man, could dim Hayes's passion for MacArthur. "To me," she said, "it was an offense against God to come between two people in love. In my arrogance, I would have stood up to the Holy Father himself."

In fact, MacArthur was not a divorced man at this point. Although his estranged wife had agreed to end the marriage, MacArthur's newfound celebrity apparently put him in a new light, and she made the divorce proceedings long and difficult. When MacArthur finally won his freedom, his ex-wife exploded with rage. "I wouldn't have Charlie MacArthur if he came in a box of Cracker Jacks!" she told reporters. "I would and I did," said Hayes later. "He was my prize, and now that it was possible legally, I refused to let anything keep us apart."

The MacArthur-Hayes courtship had placed the couple in the spotlight, making them "the most sought-after sovereigns along the White Way," according to syndicated columnist Walter Winchell. "Everybody, but ev-

*The MacArthurs embrace soon after their front-page "secret wedding."
Hayes might not be contented with him, warned MacArthur, but she
would never be bored.*

erybody, was dying to gawk at this diverse pair," noted playwright George S. Kaufman. Tired of the relentless publicity, Hayes and MacArthur decided on a secret wedding. On August 17, 1928, accompanied by Essie Brown and Alexander Woollcott, the couple went to the office of a Manhattan judge who had promised a quick, discreet ceremony. When they got there, however, the judge was nowhere to be seen. His secretary assured them he would return shortly, but 45 minutes passed before he appeared. Even then, he continued to delay the ceremony, insisting that the nervous wedding party admire pictures of his grandchild and listen to him talk about a new investment scheme.

An hour past the scheduled time for the wedding, the judge's secretary burst into his office. "You can go ahead with the ceremony!" she shouted. "The press is here!" Unable to resist the thought of being front-page news, the judge had revealed the couple's wedding plans to every newspaper in town. MacArthur and Hayes fumed, but Woollcott was amused. "Every woman," he said, "should once in her life be married to Charles MacArthur."

Ten minutes later, their nuptial vows spoken, Helen and Charles MacArthur swept past the crowd of reporters and headed for their wedding supper at a friend's apartment. On her way to the theater afterward, Hayes heard a newsboy peddling his papers. "Read all about it!" he yelled. "Read all about the secret wedding of Helen Hayes and Charles MacArthur!" Hayes was probably thinking of what her new husband had just told her: "I may never be able to give you contentment, but I promise you'll never be bored." She never doubted the word of the man she once described as "playwright and playboy, reporter and soldier of fortune, blazing wit and the eternal, white-haired boy— my Charlie."

Hayes's Madelon contemplates life in the 1931 film The Sin of Madelon Claudet. *Playing a French prostitute represented a sharp departure for Hayes, but the role earned her an Oscar.*

FIVE

"First Lady of the American Theater"

For Hayes and MacArthur, 1928 was a banner year: They celebrated not only their marriage but individual professional success. MacArthur had his first Broadway hit as coauthor of *Lulu Belle*, an updated version of the 1845 French novel *Carmen*, and Hayes was in the midst of her most popular play to date. Two years earlier, she had scored a triumph in James Barrie's *What Every Woman Knows*, a comedy that called for her to speak with a rich Scottish burr. As Barrie's wistful heroine, Maggie Wylie, Hayes delighted both public and critics. John Mason Brown of the New York *Evening Post*, for example, said, "Hayes lights up the whole play and brings out of it the enchantments of pure magic." Originally scheduled for a limited 4-week run, *What Every Woman Knows* played for 58 weeks on Broadway before embarking on a sold-out national tour.

After *What Every Woman Knows*, Hayes found herself pursued by every producer on Broadway. She finally signed up for *Coquette*, an emotional tale of doomed love in the Deep South. Hayes played Norma Besant, a flirtatious young woman whose possessive father kills the man she loves. According to the original script, Norma reacts to the murder only by weeping for her dead lover, but Hayes refused to play it that way. If she were in Norma's situation, she said, she would want revenge, not pity. The producer and director emphatically disagreed. Hayes rarely displayed "star temperament," but this time she dug in her heels. In the end, she played Norma her way.

When it opened on Broadway in November 1927, *Coquette* electrified theatergoers. The play's—and Hayes's—big moment came at the end of the second act: Learning of her father's

Osgood Perkins (right) and Lee Tracy star in The Front Page, *the riotous Charles MacArthur–Ben Hecht comedy about life on a Chicago newspaper.*

murderous deed, Norma pounds her fist into a couch and screams, "I hope he hangs, I hope he hangs!" As the curtain fell, audience members forgot their sophisticated Manhattan manners as they rocked the theater with shouts of "Hayes, Hayes, Hayes!" Speaking for most observers, author Noël Coward wrote, "Helen Hayes gave an astonishingly perfect performance. She ripped our emotions to shreds."

On August 14, 1928, *Coquette* producer Jed Harris closed his wildly successful show—but only for one night. He darkened the theater so his star could attend the opening of a very important play: *The Front Page*, by

Charles MacArthur and Ben Hecht. At this point, MacArthur and Hayes had not yet set a date for their wedding; the prospective groom had announced that he could not marry until he had written "a really significant" play. *The Front Page*, a riotously funny view of life on a Chicago newspaper, appeared to be that play. As applause, shouts, whistles, and cheers followed the final curtain, MacArthur turned to Hayes and shouted, "Will you marry me?" Three days later, the couple stood in the office of a New York City judge, vowing to love and honor one another forever.

After living in a hotel for several months, Hayes and her husband bought an apartment on Manhattan's fashionable East Side. Between *Coquette* and *The Front Page*—which had been sold to Hollywood for an enormous sum— the couple had plenty of money. Despite Hayes's assurances to her mother, she and her husband decided to have a baby. In August 1929, when she reached Los Angeles on tour with *Coquette*, Hayes was three months pregnant. Her elated husband had only one request: "Make sure it's a girl." But the strain of cross-country travel and nightly performances had begun to take their toll on Hayes; after she fainted in Los Angeles, her doctor ordered her to quit the show and rest until the baby arrived.

When Jed Harris closed his now starless play, other cast members demanded severance pay. Harris replied that, according to the contract, he was not obliged to pay severance if the play closed because of fire, accident, or an

Hayes and MacArthur show off their daughter, Mary, born on February 15, 1930. Reporters playfully nicknamed Mary the Act of God Baby.

"act of God," which surely applied to the birth of a baby. To the distress of Hayes, who had hoped to keep her pregnancy private, Hollywood columnists and reporters pounced on the story, tagging her unborn child the Act of God Baby. After Actors' Equity ruled that the cast members must be paid, a local newspaper ran a cartoon showing a plump stork atop a pile of money. "MacArthur Baby not an Act of God," read the caption. Hayes was not especially pleased, but her husband roared with laughter. "At last," he said, "I'm getting some of the credit."

On February 15, 1930, Hayes gave birth to her child in New York City. Just as the baby's father had ordered, the new arrival was a girl, named Mary by her proud parents. According to friends on the scene, Charles MacArthur's first words about his daughter were: "Why, she's more beautiful than the Brooklyn Bridge!" Then he went out and bought her a bunch of violets. "We have given her life and death, Helen," he told his wife. "That's all we can be sure of."

When Mary was a year old, her parents decided to move to California. They thought fresh air and sunshine would be good for her; besides, MacArthur already had a movie-script assignment, and Hayes had received several offers from film producers. The actress had mixed emotions about going to Hollywood. A film career seemed like a glamorous and exciting prospect, but a real movie star, she thought, should be statuesque and gorgeous. "I wasn't something for the boys. I wasn't tall, long-legged, broad-shouldered or deep-bosomed like Joan Crawford. I didn't have Garbo's hollows under my cheekbones," she said. "Everything about me was ordinary."

Hollywood did not agree. Irving Thalberg, MGM's powerful production chief, immediately offered Hayes the lead in *Lullaby*, a film about a French prostitute named Madelon Claudet. Hayes, usually cast as a sweet, innocent young woman, was thrilled. Madelon, a country girl who becomes a hard-boiled streetwalker, tender mother, and, finally, a pitiful derelict, was a role she could get her teeth into. But despite her enthusiasm, and despite her husband's last-minute rewrite of the script, the finished film pleased no one. After a screening for the press, one industry paper summed up the film community's reaction: "Miss Hayes," said the newspaper, "should never have left Broadway." MGM officials decided not to release *Lullaby*.

Meanwhile, producer Samuel Goldwyn saw the film and decided Hayes would be perfect for the lead in his new movie, *Arrowsmith*, based on Sinclair Lewis's best-selling 1925 novel. Hayes was doubtful about making another movie; she preferred working in the theater, where she knew her way around and where she felt assured of at least some success. Still, the *Arrowsmith* project was attractive, and she hated to leave Hollywood with nothing to balance the failure of *Lullaby*. As it turned out, *Arrowsmith* more than made up for the earlier disappointment. Released in late 1931, it received glowing reviews: Hayes, wrote one critic, "makes our Garbos, Dietrichs, Shearers, and Swansons, clever though they may be, look like amateurs."

While Hayes was filming *Arrowsmith*, Irving Thalberg took a long look at *Lullaby*. The movie, he decided, had some serious flaws, but these could be corrected with a few days of additional shooting. He ordered the revisions, re-named the film *The Sin of Madelon Claudet*, and invited the press to view it. Crushed by the reception of the movie's first version, Hayes and Mac-Arthur skipped the screening and went to visit friends. Late that night, Hayes got an excited phone call from a studio executive: "Helen, I love you!" he said. "The revised film is a pure gem. The audience ate it up and kept shouting for

Weary and ashamed, the unmarried Madelon (Hayes) refuses to look at her newborn child. Such wrenching scenes helped make The Sin of Madelon Claudet *a box-office hit.*

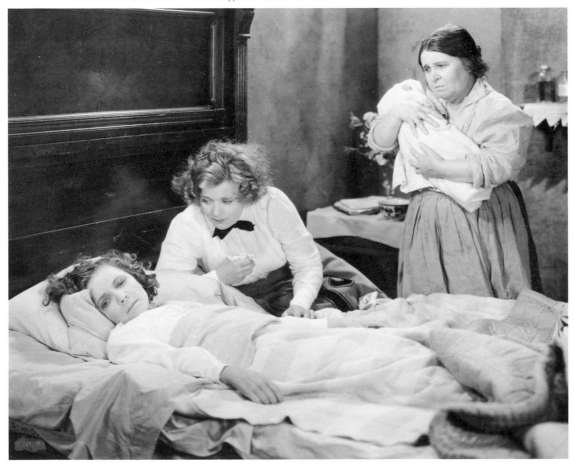

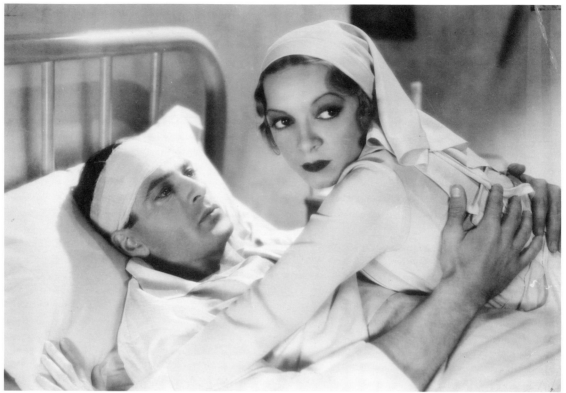

Catherine Barkley (Hayes) embraces Frederic Henry (Gary Cooper) in A Farewell to Arms. *Most contemporary critics believe the 1932 film to be Hayes's best.*

the star. I always knew you were a 110 percent genius!''

Hayes and her husband responded in good Hollywood style: They leapt, fully dressed, into their friends' swimming pool. "I always knew my wife had 110 percent talent," bellowed a dripping, delighted MacArthur. Critics and audiences agreed. *The Sin of Madelon Claudet*, said one reviewer, offered "the finest exhibition of sheer artistry the cinema has seen in seasons. Possibly it has been equaled; never has it been excelled.''

Moviegoers across the United States and Europe flocked to see *Madelon*, which MGM advertised in the overheated language of early filmdom: "She Sank to the Very Depths—But in the End She Kept the Secret Locked in Her Heart. Introducing to the Screen one of America's Greatest Stage Stars." Hayes's Madelon won her an Academy Award as best actress of 1931–32, making her the first stage actress so honored.

In her next film, *A Farewell to Arms*, Hayes costarred with a tall young actor named Gary Cooper. Based on Ernest Hemingway's celebrated 1929 novel, the movie recounts the tragic love affair between an English nurse and an American ambulance driver during World War I. Although the stars' difference in height inspired a few wisecracks—one critic called the film "the best portrayal of a romance between a giant and a dwarf"—*A Farewell to Arms* brought Hayes an avalanche of praise. Many modern film observers, in fact, consider it her best film. When it opened in 1932, New York movie reviewer Richard Watts said the "haunting beauty" of Hayes's doomed nurse introduced "qualities of splendor" not present in Hemingway's novel.

Despite such acclaim, Hollywood was not sure what to do with the distinctly unglamorous Hayes. Screen makeup artists did their best to make her look like a star, giving her long false eyelashes, elaborately styled hairdos, and artificially bow-shaped lips. Still, film executives fretted. "Have you any sex appeal at all?" asked MGM chief Louis B. Mayer. "If only you had a face like Garbo. Then we could cope with all this great acting." The actress knew his efforts to transform her were fruitless. No matter what he did, she told him, "I'll still look like Helen Hayes." Hollywood puzzled Hayes as much as she puzzled it. "It's such an odd, limited sort of life," she wrote later. "You spend all day making films; then if you go to a dinner party you talk all the way through the meal about films. After dinner the women are all segregated, often for the rest of the

evening, so that the men can talk among themselves. About films."

Hollywood parties made Hayes uncomfortable for another reason: her husband's drinking. Hayes would adore her "Charlie" for the rest of his life, treasuring his high-spirited charm, his gentleness, and his generosity. Sometimes, however, she found her patience

MacArthur and Hayes attend a Hollywood premiere in 1934. At this point, Hayes was disenchanted with life in the film capital: No one ever talked about anything, she said, but movies.

Wearing Hollywood-style Chinese makeup, Ramon Navarro (left), Lewis Stone, and Hayes play a scene from The Son-Daughter, *a 1933 movie described by one critic as "junk."*

can't be expected to watch him destroy himself." But she always changed her mind. "I was much more honest," she said, "when I announced, 'If I ever threaten to leave you, Charlie, take no notice. . . . You'll have to shoot me to get rid of me.' "

But no matter how she felt about Hollywood and its effect on her husband, Hayes had signed a movie contract, and she kept making movies. In 1933, the New York *Herald Tribune* called her "literally role-proof . . . the only actress now on the American screen who does not need to worry about what they cast her in." Her next two movies, however, suggested otherwise. In *The Son-Daughter*, she played a long-suffering Chinese matron (complete with taped, "Oriental" eyes) who strangles her evil husband with his own pigtail. "A piece of junk," said one of the kinder critics.

Hayes followed this box-office disaster with *White Sister*, a 1933 melodrama in which she played a woman who joins a convent after hearing that her lover is dead. The lover—played by Clark Gable—returns to claim her, but she nobly sends him off, after which he really dies. Not even Hayes and Gable could do much with this one. The actress, said critic Richard Watts, was "lovely" but not "effective emotionally."

Hollywood's early producers churned out films at a far faster pace than today's filmmakers. In one six-month period, Hayes made not only *A Farewell to Arms*, *The Son-Daughter*, and *The White Sister* but also the well-received

strained by his constant imbibing, his unpredictable behavior, and his readiness to swing at anyone who annoyed him. At one party, for example, Hayes noticed him deep in conversation with David Selznick, a film mogul he detested. "Do you think it's all right for your husband to be talking to David?" asked a friend. Hayes replied that the two seemed to be "getting along like a house on fire," but a minute later, they were trading punches on the floor. MacArthur let up only when Selznick's wife began pounding his head with her spike-heeled shoe. Always a joker, MacArthur rubbed his bruised head, laughed, and said, "Now I know why I like women who wear flat shoes."

After such occasions, Hayes wrote later, she would think, "I'm through. I

Hayes appears in Maxwell Anderson's 1933 play Mary of Scotland. *To portray history's tallest queen, said the diminutive Hayes, she learned to think* tall.

Another Language and *Night Flight*, in which she once again costarred with Clark Gable. By this time—mid-1933—Hayes knew it was time to return to Broadway, where an intriguing project awaited her. Essie Brown, who still read scripts submitted to her daughter, had just come up with a winner: *Mary of Scotland*, by Maxwell Anderson.

At first, Hayes was doubtful about her ability to play Anderson's heroine. Mary Stuart, queen of Scotland, cousin of Queen Elizabeth I of England, and a claimant to the British throne, had been more than six feet tall. Hayes barely topped five feet. The actors already cast as Elizabeth and as Mary's husband were both very tall. Finally, deciding she would learn to *think* tall for the role, Hayes accepted it. "My posture became military," she recalled. "I became the tallest five-foot woman in the world. And my refusal to be limited by my limitations enabled me to play Mary of Scotland, the tallest queen in history."

Mary provided Hayes with a new triumph. "Never in a career that began with her childhood and has included many successes," wrote critic Burns Mantle, "has this actress approached the quality of this particular performance." Playing the gallant, ill-fated queen (beheaded by order of her royal cousin in 1587) gave Hayes a chance to stretch the skills she had been developing for the last 25 years. Still, she was not always happy with her work. Even after playing Mary hundreds of times, she recalled later, she felt "a twinge of dissatisfaction about it." Then, on tour

with the play in Columbus, Ohio, she experienced an unforgettable evening. She told biographer Kenneth Barrow (*Helen Hayes: First Lady of the American Theatre*) about it:

> On that particular night I couldn't have felt drearier. I'd rather have been anywhere than in the theater. I was . . . feeling lonely and tired and too far away from Charlie and Mary. My cue came. . . . Then it happened. Mary Stuart spoke through me with all her strength, gentleness, and simple dignity. I played as if I were in a trance. . . . I had never given such a performance as Mary in New York and I never gave such a performance again. . . . That night was the kind of experience an actor lives for.

To fulfill her Hollywood contract, Hayes made two more pictures, but her heart was not in her work. "I asked myself why I was persisting in the movies," she wrote later. "And I had to confess to myself that I had become enslaved to that great big paycheck, to the neglect of my home, my family, and my own life." Talking with a reporter when she left Hollywood, Hayes said, "I don't think I'm much good in pictures and I have a beautiful dream that I'm elegant on the stage."

Returning to the East Coast for good in 1935, Hayes and MacArthur bought a house in Nyack, New York, the Hudson River town where MacArthur had grown up. The family settled happily into "Pretty Penny," Hayes's name for the expensive but beautiful old house with its trees, broad green lawns, and sweeping views of the river. Here, five-year-old Mary could roam safely, and here too, Hayes and MacArthur hoped to raise more children. After years of tests, however, they discovered that Hayes was unable to have another baby, and in 1937 they adopted a son, James Gordon MacArthur.

Only 27 miles from Manhattan, Nyack suited Hayes perfectly; she could work in the theater and still enjoy a relaxed country atmosphere with her family. Life with MacArthur remained as unpredictable as ever: "Living with him made me shock-proof," Hayes once wrote. "He turned me, over the years, into a woman who could take anything." She liked to tell the story of one of her husband's trips from Los Angeles to New York. He decided to make the journey, "not by train, but for some mysterious reason through the Panama Canal," she re-

Seven-year-old Mary MacArthur and her famous mother descend the broad steps of "Pretty Penny," the MacArthurs' handsome 18-room home in Nyack, New York.

MacArthur and Hayes attend a Manhattan costume party in 1937. "Charlie," said Hayes, "conquered New York with the irresistible flash and sparkle of an exploding Roman candle."

66

called. "When the ship landed in Havana [Cuba], Charlie went ashore and toured the bars. When he returned to the dock, heaven knows how much later, the ship was gone."

MacArthur, Hayes said, then wired a friend for money, took a ship to Miami, and called home. He asked Hayes to meet him at New York City's Penn Station with an overcoat and boots. "Of course, I did," she recalled. Travelers at the station stared hard at Hayes, at the time seven months pregnant with Mary, and then at her husband, neatly attired in lightweight tennis clothes on the coldest day of the year. "Charlie," noted Hayes happily, "was irrepressible."

Always a hard drinker, by turns playful and cynical, dutiful and unreliable, MacArthur never deviated from one constant: He adored his wife and children. His affection sometimes emerged as prankish humor. One day at the dinner table, he told Mary it was time she learned to shoot mashed potatoes. When everyone at the table is bored, he said, a person should load a spoon with potatoes, turn the spoon around, give it a flick of the wrist, and . . . fire! Demonstrating as he spoke, MacArthur accidentally landed a direct hit on Mary's dignified governess. The startled woman took the barrage gracefully, and soon all three were roaring with laughter. "How could Mary not have adored this playmate?" asked Hayes.

Soon after she and her family moved to Nyack, Hayes brought her smash hit, *Victoria Regina*, to Broadway. In September 1937, after 517 performances, she went on a 10-month tour with the show, playing in 45 cities and towns from Connecticut to California. Already admired for her movies and for the popular weekly radio show she had begun in 1935, Hayes took the country by storm with her Queen Victoria. The show earned $2,623,031, truly a queen's ransom in the depths of the Great Depression.

When *Victoria Regina* opened in Washington, D.C., Hayes received a dinner invitation from Eleanor Roosevelt, wife of the president. Hayes was already seated with the Roosevelts' daughter and Secretary of State Cordell Hull when tall, imposing Franklin Roosevelt entered the dining room on the arm of an aide. Smiling, he looked down at the diminutive actress. "And how is your majesty?" asked the president of the United States.

At 37, Hayes had reached heights attained by few women or men in the theater. Greta Garbo, Marlene Dietrich, Lillian Gish, and other leading ladies had their ardent fans, but for many people, Hayes was in a class by herself. "How splendid that she is known as the First Lady of the American Theater," commented her fellow actress, Dame Flora Robson. "It is an accolade she alone deserves." But the grand title made Hayes uncomfortable. Referring to her many saintly roles, she once laughingly suggested "the Holy Cow" as a more appropriate nickname for herself, "particularly when overweight." Hayes claimed that she did

Mary MacArthur sketches a portrait of her mother as Queen Victoria. Looking on is 15-month-old James Gordon MacArthur, adopted by Hayes and her husband in 1937.

her best to be a "prima donna," especially during the run of *Victoria*, but that she found it hard to take herself that seriously. "It's a pity," she joked. "I had learned to be an actress; I never learned to be a star."

As though to prove the point, Hayes sometimes told the story of a trip she had made to the Greek island of Mykonos. When she arrived, the landlady of her hotel greeted her with obvious adoration. "I was pregnant and saw you in *Broken Blossoms*," gushed the hotelkeeper, "and I sat in the dark praying that the child would be like you and she is and I'm so grateful." Hayes added that she spent the remainder of her time on the island "avoiding this woman, so she'd never discover that I wasn't Lillian Gish."

Hayes (left) costars with Maurice Evans in a 1940 production of Shakespeare's comedy Twelfth Night. *Hayes, 40, earned critical cheers for her portrayal of the teenage Viola.*

S I X

Milestones

ILOVE YOU I LOVE YOU I LOVE YOU I LOVE YOU I LOVE YOU I LOVE YOU I LOVE YOU I LOVE YOU I LOVE YOU I LOVE YOU, read the wire from superstar Gertrude Lawrence. GREETINGS TO THE MOST EXCITING OF ALL ACTRESSES, said Katharine Hepburn's cable. These and scores of other telegrams, all wishing Hayes luck, covered her backstage dressing table. The curtain would soon go up on Hayes's new play, a Hungarian comedy called *Ladies and Gentlemen*. Her first show since the dazzling *Victoria Regina*, it had been adapted for Hayes by Charles MacArthur and Ben Hecht. Hayes liked the play, which gave her the chance to play a comic secretary after several years of impersonating a solemn queen. But her fans, who had expected to see her in another majestic role, expressed vast disappointment, and critics denounced the play itself: "Trashy," said one.

Not a complete disaster, *Ladies and Gentlemen* survived to enjoy a four-

month run on Broadway, then went on tour. When the show reached Cincinnati, Ohio, in March 1940, Hayes received sad news: Her father had died. Frank Brown spent his last years in a house his daughter had bought for him, on Maryland's Chesapeake Bay. He had loved his house and garden, had often visited Hayes and her family in Nyack, and had taken great pride in his daughter's career and "unactressish" private life. Hayes had often gently teased him about his strong southern accent. "I was told," she recalled after his death, "that my father used to boast that 'mah daughtah nevah has appeahed in a piece that was impropuh.'" The actress grieved for her father, but she was comforted by knowing he had enjoyed the last part of his life. "He had found his peace," she said.

A few months after her father's death, Hayes opened in Shakespeare's comedy *Twelfth Night*. Playing the

Charles MacArthur (left) confers with colleague Ben Hecht in the early 1940s. Columnists tagged the inseparable duo "Broadway's mischievous Siamese twins."

teenage Viola, the 40-year-old actress earned a critical reception that more than made up for *Ladies and Gentlemen*'s lukewarm reviews: Her performance, said Richard Watts, was one of "sweet and tender loveliness . . . lyric, warm, human, humorous, and incredibly moving." A few observers complained that Hayes's "conversational" delivery of Shakespeare's lines robbed the play of its poetry, but most approved of her natural style. "She made Viola into the kind of human being everyone knows," said one admirer.

Hayes followed Viola with a portrayal of Madeleine Guest, the central character in Maxwell Anderson's patriotic play *Candle in the Wind*. Two months after the play's October 1941 opening, the Japanese bombed the U.S. naval base at Pearl Harbor, Hawaii, and America entered World War II. Charles MacArthur, already a veteran of two wars, immediately enlisted in the U.S. Army. Commissioned a major in the Chemical Corps, he was sent to Europe; there, his friends joked, the hard-drinking playwright would probably serve as a secret weapon. "They'll fly over Berlin holding him head over heels," insisted one crony. "Then when he breathes on the city, it will collapse."

When MacArthur actually did participate in a bombing run over the German capital, he handed the bombardier an armful of empty whiskey bottles. "Drop them on the German high command," he ordered. Traveling through other war areas for the Chemical Corps, MacArthur carried the usual identification papers. In the space for "person to notify in case of accident," he wrote the name of President Harry Truman. "Officials the world over," he gleefully reported, "practically fell on their beaks trying to be helpful." On his return from the war, MacArthur tossed a small bag into his wife's lap. It contained several uncut emeralds from India. "I wish they were peanuts," he said.

Despite MacArthur's flippant attitude, he had been deeply disturbed by the war. "He seemed overwhelmed by the senselessness of the killing and destruction," said his colleague Ben Hecht. "He'd write frequent passages about how simple and kind the world should be. Then he'd rip them out of his typewriter and send them sailing on the river." Hayes knew there were two people who could always relieve MacArthur's somber moods: his beloved children. "Charlie was a good father," she recalled later. "Mary and Jamie adored him—and why wouldn't they have? He shared with all other children the love of the outrageous."

Hayes enjoys a backstage chat with her husband, now Major Charles MacArthur, before he heads overseas during World War II. MacArthur emerged from the war as a lieutenant colonel.

In later years, Hayes chuckled over a bit of Jamie's outrageousness, inspired by his father. On the way home from lunch at a fashionable restaurant, she realized she had forgotten her glasses. Leaving her husband and son outside, the nondrinking actress went in to ask the restaurant bartender if anyone had turned in the glasses. At this point, young Jamie, coached by his father, raced into the restaurant. "Please! Please!" he wailed. "Don't give my mother another drink!"

Neither Hayes nor MacArthur encouraged their children to pursue careers in the theater, but the "acting

Helen (right), Charles, and Mary MacArthur cuddle up in the mid-1940s. An adoring father, MacArthur once described his daughter as "more beautiful than the Brooklyn Bridge."

bug," as Hayes put it, bit both children early. Mary had made her debut at the age of six, when she had been allowed a brief walk-on part during one of her mother's performances as Queen Victoria. At about the same age, Jamie had also made a stage appearance, this one unrehearsed. Backstage watching his mother perform one day, Jamie heard her cry out, "My son! Where is my son?" Unaware that this was one of Hayes's lines, the little boy rushed onstage, shouting, "Mommy! Here I am!" The play's serious mood was broken, but the audience loved it.

Jamie would follow in his mother's footsteps, becoming a highly successful actor. A star of the long-running television series "Hawaii Five-O," James MacArthur has appeared in dozens of movies, stage plays, and television shows. Mary, too, showed early promise as an actress. In 1946, she costarred with her mother in James Barrie's *Alice-Sit-by-the-Fire* at a community theater in Pennsylvania. "The night we opened I lost myself watching the magic flare up in Mary's eyes as she spoke to me on stage," recalled Hayes. "Mary had the star on her forehead." The veteran actress admitted that acting with her daughter made her so excited that she forgot her own lines. Mary, she said, had to prompt her.

Mary MacArthur went from costarring with her mother to touring with actress Lillian Gish. When Gish asked if Hayes had any instructions for taking care of 17-year-old Mary, Hayes said, "No. She'll take care of you." Meanwhile, Hayes went on to her own next

play, *Happy Birthday*. A comedy by Anita Loos, *Happy Birthday* provided the actress with an entirely new kind of role. Explaining the plot to her, Loos said it was about Addie Beamis, "a frustrated teetotaler [abstainer from alcohol] who resents anybody having fun. But one evening, she gets gloriously tight and, during a 12-hour bender, turns into such a sympathetic human being that she straightens out her life and lands the husband of her dreams." Or, as MacArthur put it, "a sort of Cinderella with booze."

Hayes wrote later that she "had a ball as Addie Beamis," and critics shared her pleasure. Describing her performance after the play's October 1946 opening, reviewer George Freedley said, "She dances in the spotlight [and] bops her poor old father over the head with a liquor bottle. . . . In other words Our Helen had an evening for herself and audiences are going to like her better than ever." Freedley was right. *Happy Birthday* ran for 564 performances and earned Hayes the first Antoinette Perry (Tony) Award as best actress of the year.

Four months later, Hayes made her first appearance in London, playing Amanda Wingfield in Tennessee Williams's *The Glass Menagerie*. The role had been originated by actress Laurette Taylor, but Taylor had died before she could bring the show to London. Her last wish had been that Hayes take over the part. Hayes heartily disliked both the play and the role, but she had idolized Taylor and felt obliged to honor her final request.

Hayes helps her daughter rehearse for Alice-Sit-by-the-Fire, *the James Barrie play in which they costarred in 1946. "Mary," said Hayes later, "had the star on her forehead."*

Despite her distaste for the play, Hayes scored a smash hit in her London debut. "She fulfills all I feel about acting—she has restored my faith," said the distinguished British actress Dame Sybil Thorndike. "Never for one moment does she let you see the wheels working, though they are oiled marvelously." Still loathing the play, Hayes gave 109 successful performances as Amanda. Ironically, it became one of her most popular roles; over the following decades, she would appear in *The Glass Menagerie* more often than in any other play.

Soon after her return from England, Hayes began a pre-Broadway tour in *Good Housekeeping*, a light comedy costarring her daughter. The two actresses were having a wonderful time with their joint venture until Mary came down with a bad cold. Her mother insisted that she take a few days off to rest, but the young actress failed to improve. Deciding that she had influenza, her doctor sent her to New York's Lenox Hill Hospital. At first, Mary's illness puzzled her doctors, but within a few days they made a terrifying diagnosis: Mary had been stricken by polio, or infantile paralysis, the crippling, often fatal disease that periodically swept the nation's young people.

When MacArthur telephoned Hayes with the grim news, she closed her show and rushed to the hospital. There, she found her daughter in an iron lung, a mechanical device designed to aid the breathing of paralyzed polio victims. As Hayes and MacArthur gazed down

Playing the newly "liberated" Addie Beamis in Anita Loos's 1947 comedy Happy Birthday, *Hayes cuts up as Grace Valentine (center) and Enid Markey smile approvingly.*

at their beautiful daughter, she smiled, wiggled her toes, and said, "Let's the three of us get out of here." Moments later, she gasped in pain and murmured, "Help me, Pops."

Disguising her anguish with simple, unadorned words, Hayes later wrote: "It isn't natural to outlive one's child. It is against everything natural, but it happens. It happened to us. Our Mary lost her battle a few days later. She was 19." Mary MacArthur died of polio on September 22, 1949.

"Helen had always been small," said an old friend who visited her after Mary's funeral, "but that night she was

Essie Brown (above, in 1940) died in 1952. "If my stage-struck mother hadn't catapulted me into the theater," said Hayes, "I'd never have had . . . all the richness in my life."

shriveled, shrunk, pitiful." Fearing for her sanity, MacArthur desperately tried to convince Hayes to take on a new play, but she said she could not manage it. He finally persuaded her to join him on a trip to Hawaii, hoping that travel would help them both. "Charlie became stronger than he had ever been when he saw me sway," Hayes wrote many years later. "He became my bastion until I regained my balance." The couple did their best to appreciate Hawaii, but nothing could dim their sorrow.

MacArthur later told a friend about the day he had seen a pair of sunglasses in a Honolulu shop window. "They'll be just right for Mary," he said to himself. Not until he was back in the street, glasses in hand, did he realize what he had done. Then, noting a young woman about Mary's age, he thrust the glasses into her hands and raced away. "I never told Helen about it. How could I?" said MacArthur. "Those two were so close."

Hayes had no heart for a return to the stage. She even talked of retirement. But after much persuasion, she agreed to appear in *The Wisteria Trees*, a new adaptation of Russian author Anton Chekhov's *The Cherry Orchard*. Reviewers criticized the play, which transferred the action from Russia to the American South, but they welcomed Hayes back to the stage. And the project proved helpful, leading her to other projects and, eventually, to her acceptance of life without Mary.

In October 1950, Hayes tackled a fresh professional challenge: television.

At first suspicious of the new medium ("Television will mean the end of all art in the theater," she had said in the late 1940s), she soon became its advocate. Although she found TV "a little more hurried" than the stage, she saw it as "alive and rewarding, at least from an actor's point of view." Before the end of 1951, she had appeared in six television dramas, including condensed versions of *Victoria Regina* and *Mary of Scotland*. In later years, she happily accepted small television roles. Theater fans would not approve of a star accepting anything but a leading role, Hayes pointed out, but "on television, the biggest stars play small parts. They're not trying to hold up the universe every time."

In 1952, Hayes returned to the stage as the rich, insufferably snobbish Mrs. Howard V. Larue II in Mary Chase's fantasy-comedy *Mrs. McThing*. After she offends the daughter of a witch, Mrs. Larue finds herself transformed into a maid, an experience that eventually teaches her some wisdom. Hayes brought down the house when, as Mrs. Larue, she ineptly tried to sweep a floor. "Miss Hayes's ingenious magic is in full bloom here," wrote critic William Hawkins. "She is staggeringly funny, aiming to please with a broom." A smash hit, *Mrs. McThing* played to packed houses for more than a year.

Among those applauding on *Mrs. McThing*'s opening night was 76-year-old Essie Brown, as ever her daughter's most loyal fan. But that play was the last she ever saw; Brown died the following summer. Although she had

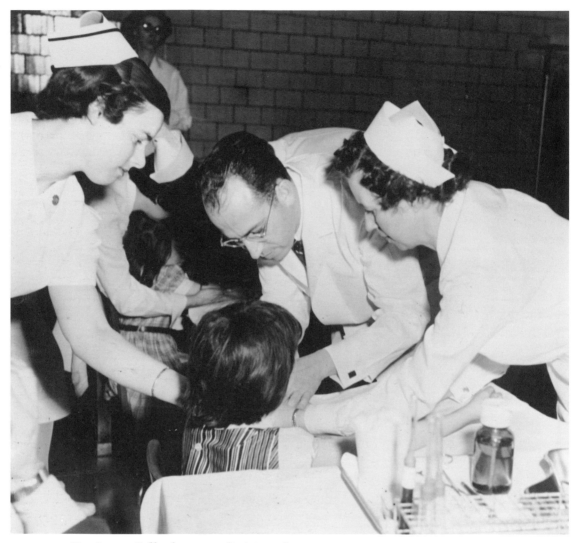

Dr. Jonas Salk shows technicians how to immunize patients against polio. After the disease killed her daughter, Hayes helped educate the public about Salk's lifesaving vaccine.

sometimes bullied and often distressed her beloved daughter, Essie Brown had played a large part in making her a star, a debt Hayes never forgot. Overall, she said, "Mother's great capacity for love outweighed everything else."

Hayes would always grieve for her own daughter, but she gradually came to see that she could best honor Mary by attacking the disease that had killed her. "I was struck by the fact," she wrote, "that if there is any divinity, it is in man's willingness to help alleviate suffering in others. . . . I knew without the slightest doubt that Mary could continue to help cheer others, and I knew that this would please her happy spirit."

When the March of Dimes Foundation, an organization formed to fight polio, asked Hayes to chair its national volunteer program, she accepted. And when medical researcher Jonas Salk developed a vaccine that would begin to eliminate polio, he asked Hayes to help persuade the nation's parents to immunize their children. She accepted, speaking to frightened children and suspicious parents across the country. Hayes, said Dr. Salk, had been his "most valuable weapon" in the battle to overcome public fear of his lifesaving vaccine.

In her 1990 autobiography, *My Life in Three Acts*, Hayes asserts, "I'm not a leader and never have been the inspiration behind anything." Although Hayes's dramatic skills have rarely been disputed, most observers found this statement unconvincing: In some cases, perhaps, Hayes's actions have spoken louder than her words.

Broadway's tribute to its "First Lady" lights up the night. The Fulton Theatre became the Helen Hayes in 1955, 50 years after the actress's first stage appearance.

SEVEN

"A Walking Legend"

For once, no one noticed her. A small figure, warmly dressed against the November wind, Helen Hayes stood alone in front of Manhattan's Fulton Theatre at Broadway and 46th Street. As she looked on, workmen lowered the theater's old sign and prepared to hoist a new one. It read: HELEN HAYES THEATRE. Hayes later told biographer Kenneth Barrow that she cried then, thinking of how thrilled her mother would have been at that moment. The renaming of the theater marked Hayes's golden anniversary as an actress: 50 years earlier, she had played Peaseblossom in *A Midsummer Night's Dream*. Seeing her name on a theater, Hayes said later, "made me feel somewhat unreal, as though I'd become a walking legend."

Indeed, the theater world regarded her as just that. In late 1955, Broadwayites honored the half-century reign of their "First Lady" with a nonstop run of parties, plaques, and speeches. The day before New Year's Eve, almost every major theatrical figure in New York assembled in the Grand Ballroom of the Waldorf-Astoria Hotel to watch a parade of actors dramatize Hayes's life story. Seated between her son and her husband, the actress watched with alternating tears and laughter.

After that night, MacArthur and Hayes made few public appearances together. MacArthur's health and spirits had been steadily declining since his daughter's death in 1949. Alcohol, depression, ulcers, and kidney disease all attacked him; by the summer of 1955, he knew he was dying. When Hayes showed him some renovation plans for the family home in Nyack, he said, "I'll never live to see those changes." Hayes gasped, "Charlie, you don't mean that!" But, she recalled sadly, "he did."

Even in his last illness, MacArthur showed flashes of the irreverent humor Hayes loved. During one televised in-

Hayes, costumed for her role in The Skin of Our Teeth, *and Charles MacArthur proudly watch their son's 1955 television debut. The couple saw the show in Hayes's dressing room at the ANTA Theatre.*

terview, for example, journalist Edward R. Murrow asked MacArthur to explain his philosophy of life. "A condemned man whose hanging I once covered in Chicago summed it up in four words," replied MacArthur. "As the prisoner reached the gallows steps he asked, 'Is this thing safe?'" At another point, MacArthur woke up in his hospital bed to find himself surrounded by white-coated doctors and nurses. "What the hell is this?" he bellowed. "Some kind of block party?"

But neither wit nor courage nor his wife's love could save Charlie Mac-Arthur. In and out of the hospital for months, he returned there in the spring of 1956, knowing that this time he would not survive. "I don't mind going," he told his wife. "I believe in God, Helen, and I'm not afraid. It's just this lousy exit they've written for me." Hayes sat at his bedside, holding his hands. "I love you," she whispered. He opened his eyes, winked, and spoke his last words: "You should," he said.

MacArthur had made it clear that he wanted no funeral. Teasing his wife, he had said, "If you do that to me, I'll come back and haunt you!" But Hayes knew that his friends wanted a chance to say goodbye to him, and she invited them to a memorial service soon after his death. Hundreds of journalists and theater people listened as playwright Ben Hecht eulogized his friend. Winding up his tribute, Hecht said, "His gaiety, wildness, and kindness; his love for his bride, Helen, and for his two children and for his clan of brothers and sisters; his wit and adventures will

Hayes and her son, Jim, leave Charles MacArthur's memorial service in 1956. The actress said she never regretted marrying MacArthur, "the man God picked out for me."

live a long, long while." At this point, a large floral wreath hanging behind Hecht began to sway violently. Hecht smiled, and other friends exchanged knowing looks. "Charlie," remarked one, "was having his last protest."

Recalling MacArthur's wedding day promise, that his wife might not be contented, but that she would never be bored, Hayes later wrote: "He was true to his word. There were times when I was anxious and moments when I despaired, but there was so much fun and laughter, and so much love, in between. Though we had our rough periods, they never came from . . . boredom."

Before her husband's death, Hayes had declined 20th Century-Fox's offer of a part in the upcoming film *Anastasia*. Several months later, the role of the dowager Russian empress remained unfilled, and Fox approached Hayes again. She had no desire to do the film, but friends insisted working would be the best cure for her sorrow. "You can never find another Charlie; you can never have another child," said director Josh Logan. "But you *can* . . . use that God-given talent of yours to make other people happy." Finally, Hayes gave in and signed on for the movie, costarring with Ingrid Bergman and Yul Brynner.

As Russia's dowager empress, Hayes confronts an alleged royal relative (Ingrid Bergman) in Anastasia. *Released in 1956, the film also starred actor Yul Brynner.*

Because she would be playing a Russian noblewoman, Hayes decided she should learn to speak with the proper accent. A Russian-born neighbor offered to help, taping Hayes's lines, then correcting her as she imitated the tapes. Her tutor finally satisfied, Hayes reported for work. Serving as an adviser during the filming was a former Russian countess, who congratulated Hayes on her newly acquired accent. Bergman, too, found herself impressed with Hayes. "She symbolized that quality which distinguishes a superb actor from an adequate one," said the Swedish star. "She sat around on the set of *Anastasia* and she was a sweet little woman. She stepped on the stage and suddenly she was six feet tall."

Nevertheless, the widowed actress felt unprepared to resume her career. "That's a time I flinch to look back on, because I was most unattractive," she wrote later. "Unreliable and erratic. I squabbled with directors. I had never done that before. I took umbrage [offense] at nothing at all. . . . I was nutty and that's the truth." Hayes was not happy with her performance, but, she noted in her 1990 autobiography, "at least I believed my accent was pretty good—after all, it had passed muster with two ex-members of the Russian nobility." Later, she wryly recorded the New York *Herald Tribune*'s view of her Russian empress. "Helen Hayes," said the paper's film critic, "will remind you of your old aunt in Vermont." Hayes's response: "Sometimes, you just can't win."

Returning to Nyack when she finished *Anastasia*, Hayes gave herself what she had needed all along: time to be alone, to meditate and adjust. Her thoughts turned to the Catholic church, which she had left to marry MacArthur so many years before. "I had never regretted the decision that had alienated me from the Church," she said in *On Reflection*. "I had to choose between the Church and the man God picked out for me. . . . It was my cardinal sin, loving my husband more than anything in this or any other world." Now, however, she wanted to return to the faith of her childhood, and she began conferring with a priest. He told her that she had violated a church law by marrying MacArthur, but that her life with him had not been a sin. She returned to the church, sure that her husband would have understood: "I reminded Charlie that it was going to have to take the whole Roman Catholic Church to replace him."

As the months passed, Hayes once again grew comfortable with her work. In late 1956, she agreed to assist the New York City Opera by appearing in a two-week benefit run of her least favorite play, *The Glass Menagerie*. The following year she opened in *Time Remembered*, a gentle comedy by French playwright Jean Anouilh. *Time Remembered* enjoyed a successful run of 250 performances, but it was not a period Hayes recalled with pleasure. Costarring with her were Welsh actor Richard Burton and Susan Strasberg, fresh from her success in *The Diary of*

Richard Burton, 32, and 19-year-old Susan Strasberg play a scene with Hayes in 1957's Time Remembered. *The romance between her costars, said Hayes, made the show's 30-week run "a mess."*

Anne Frank. To the distress of Hayes and the rest of the company, Strasberg and Burton fell in love—"or, more accurately," reported Hayes, "Susan fell in love with him, and he wasn't about to turn her down."

Because Hayes's and Strasberg's dressing rooms were side by side in Manhattan's Morosco Theatre, Hayes learned considerably more than she wanted to know about the stormy romance between the young actress and the older, married actor. And when Burton's wife arrived from London with the couple's baby, it was Hayes who unhappily comforted her. "My God, what a mess!" said the actress in her memoirs. To top off the general disarray, Hayes suffered a recurrence of a respiratory ailment, caused by an allergy to dust, that had bothered her on and off for years. When *Time Remembered* closed, she took a much-needed rest.

Three months later, in October 1958, Hayes opened in Eugene O'Neill's play *A Touch of the Poet*. The occasion marked Hayes's first appearance in a work by the great American playwright and her first performance in the theater that bore her name. Playing the downtrodden wife of a drunken tavern keeper, Hayes dazzled Broadway's critics: Brooks Atkinson of the *New York Times* said she helped bring the script "vigorously alive," and reviewer Whitney Bolton praised her "gift for using tiny and seemingly inconsequential things to build a creature of dimension and earthly grandeur." *A Touch of the*

Hayes portrays the mistreated wife of a tavern keeper in Eugene O'Neill's A Touch of the Poet. *The actress's 1958 performance brought her glittering reviews.*

Poet chalked up almost 300 performances.

At this stage of her life, Hayes no longer needed to bolster her reputation, nor did she need the money she earned from such long-running but exhausting Broadway shows. Still, she genuinely loved her work and rarely took long breaks. Between 1959, when *A Touch of the Poet* ended its run, and 1966, when she joined a Manhattan repertory company, Hayes appeared in nine plays, most of which went on national tours. In 1961, the U.S. State Department asked her to join a theater company that would present three great American plays to audiences around the world. She found the idea exciting, except for one thing: One of the two productions in which she was to star was Tennessee Williams's *The Glass Menagerie.* ("All I kept thinking," she confessed later, "was, 'Oh God, why me?' ")

Hayes offered a list of alternative plays; she offered to take a small role in any other production; she offered to do *anything* but play Amanda Wingfield in *The Glass Menagerie.* But the State Department stood firm, and Hayes, gritting her teeth, finally consented. Before the tour ended, she had played Williams's bedraggled southern mother in 30 countries in Europe, the Middle East, and Latin America. Hayes may have hated the role, but audiences loved her as Amanda; she received ovations all over the world.

In 1965, the State Department asked Hayes to join another government-sponsored tour, this one to play at military bases in the Far East. She enjoyed the trip, spending most of her time coaching, rehearsing, and playing scenes with American servicemen and -women, but when she reached Tokyo, an unhappy surprise awaited: The State Department had booked her to appear on Japanese television—in *The Glass Menagerie.* As it turned out, this was one time she liked being in the play. Costarring with a Japanese actress, she did her part in English while the other actress spoke in Japanese; observers

reported that despite—or perhaps because of—the mix, the production worked beautifully.

Hayes had always envied British actors and their repertory system, in which even stars took their turns playing small roles. (A repertory company is a group of actors who present a series of different plays each season.) Hungry for the freedom to play any role that interested her, she joined New York City's Phoenix-APA (Association of

Hayes enjoys a 1967 outing with her son's children, Mary, two, and Charlie, seven. "Both of my grandchildren," said Hayes, "have been blessed with distinguished names."

Nervous but game, Hayes rides an elephant for a 1967 television episode of "Tarzan." Asked why she had accepted the assignment, Hayes said simply, "Actors are crazy."

Scandal—proved more embarrassing than exciting. When she came on stage, the audience broke into long, loud applause, disrupting the performance and making the actress, she said later, "just miserable." Eventually, Hayes fans accepted her as a regular cast member, allowing her to enter without fanfare during the company's remaining three plays of the 1966–67 season. In late 1967, she took another small role, this one in a "Tarzan" TV episode whose cast included her son, James.

Not until after Hayes signed on for the "Tarzan" show did she learn that she had to make her entrance on the back of an elephant—but a gentle baby elephant, reassured the show's director. The "baby," Hayes reported later, turned out to be 10 feet tall; riding it, she said, "was like riding the Empire State Building." The elephant started out slowly, then gathered steam. "I had no idea elephants could run that fast!" said Hayes. "Pretty soon we had passed everyone in sight, and there was just me and the elephant. I hung onto the rope for dear life." Why, at the age of 67, had she gone through with the scene? "Actors are crazy," she explained serenely.

After "Tarzan," Hayes returned to New York and began rehearsing for the Phoenix-APA production of *The Show-Off,* a 1924 comedy by George Kelly. To infuse life into her character, the hero's mother-in-law, Hayes once again raided her family album. She had used her grandmother as a model for Queen Victoria; now she summoned memories of Mamie Hayes, her mother's sis-

Producing Artists) theater company in 1966. "What a beautiful thing it is, at this stage in my career, not to have to work under that terrible, terrible pressure a star feels on Broadway," she told an interviewer. "That's what I like so much in the APA, the . . . freedom and enthusiasm and exhilarating excitement."

Hayes's first repertory appearance—in a secondary role in Richard Brinsley Sheridan's 1777 comedy *The School for*

Playing Mrs. Fisher, the hero's mother-in-law, in a 1968 production of The Show-Off, *Hayes imitates her aunt Mamie's gestures and facial expressions.*

ter. "All I had to do," she said later, "was let Aunt Mamie move in." The trick worked again—this time, a bit too well: Hayes discovered that once she had invited Aunt Mamie into her head, she could not get her out.

"So completely did she take me over," recalled Hayes, "that at rehearsals, alarmingly near our opening, I was still expressing myself in her words instead of the author's." Exasperated, Hayes finally "called up to the peanut gallery [the upper balcony], which is nearest in theater to heaven, 'Okay, Aunt Mamie. Thanks for your help, but will you kindly leave the stage so I can get on with it?' The rest of the cast thought I'd gone mad!"

The Show-Off opened to critical cheers, with Hayes's mother-in-law character drawing rave notices. The comedy played for 30 weeks—a record-breaking run for repertory theater—then toured for another 14 weeks, attracting standing-room-only crowds across the country. In each city, the program for the show listed Hayes's name in alphabetical order with the other cast members. To Hayes, who cared much more about acting than she did about fame, that was as it should be.

Hayes graciously offers a guest poisoned wine in Arsenic and Old Lace. *Costarring in the television comedy about two murderous spinsters was Hayes's old friend Lillian Gish.*

EIGHT

"A Sort of Magic"

While *The Show-Off* played in Los Angeles, Hayes stayed at the home of old friends. Settling into the guest room, she noticed a copy of *Airport*, a best-selling novel recently purchased by a Hollywood studio. "That was thoughtful," Hayes recalled saying to herself, "though I would have preferred a dish of chocolates." At dinner that night, she met Ross Hunter, the producer who was about to make *Airport* into a movie. After admitting it had been his idea to place the book in Hayes's room, Hunter told the actress it contained an ideal role for her.

Before she went to bed, Hayes picked up the novel, intending to scan it for the sake of courtesy. By morning, she had read the whole book, intrigued by its fast-moving plot: A deranged man plans to blow up an airplane full of passengers, only to be foiled by a little old lady named Ada Quonsett. Hayes had to admit, she wrote later, that Mrs.

Quonsett "was a juicy part." The next day, after a little persuasion from Hunter, she agreed to take the role.

This time, Hayes needed no model; the quirky, tough-minded Ada Quonsett, she decided, was "pretty much" like herself. *Airport*, which would inspire a stream of other "disaster movies," delighted both filmgoers and critics. Wanda Hale of the *New York Daily News* concluded her rave review by asking:"And who steals the show?" The answer, of course, was Helen Hayes. One of the year's highest-grossing films, *Airport* received several Oscar nominations, including one for best supporting actress. Hayes wound up being the first female star to win Academy Awards both for best actress (1931–32, *The Sin of Madelon Claudet*) and best supporting actress (1970, *Airport*). She was stunned to learn she had won the Oscar. "I thought they had made a mistake," she told reporters later. But she added happily, "God bless those people in Hollywood."

The actress disliked watching her own movies, but this time she made an exception. Seated in Manhattan's Radio City Music Hall, she had just seen *Airport*'s opening credits when a man behind her exclaimed, "Helen Hayes? My God, she must be a hundred!" "I turned around and gave him a dirty look," Hayes reported afterward, "but my God, *he* looked a hundred! And I don't sass my elders."

Between *Airport*'s filming and its release, Hayes took on a new role in an old play. For six weeks in the fall of 1969, she played Mrs. Grant in a revival of *The Front Page*, the Charles MacArthur–Ben Hecht comic gem of 1928. MacArthur, who had created the cranky, nagging Grant character, had based her on a woman he knew all too well: Essie Brown. "Of course, [Mother] knew that she was portrayed as Mrs. Grant," recalled Hayes in her 1990 autobiography. "She never let on, but she *knew*." In the 40 years since its premiere, *The Front Page* had become a classic, often revived in the United States, performed in many languages all over the world, and turned into two major films. The 1969 version was hailed as perhaps the best yet, and Hayes won new praise for playing her own mother.

After portraying Essie Brown, Hayes appeared as a sweet, cheerful murderer. This time, she costarred with her old friend Lillian Gish in a television production of *Arsenic and Old Lace*, a comedy about a pair of elderly spinsters whose hobby is poisoning their visitors. The show was filmed in Brooklyn. One day, still attired in her character's long, lace-trimmed gown and bonnet, Hayes took a stroll between takes. As she concentrated on "getting into" her part, a car suddenly pulled up beside her. "Do you always go around dressed like that?" asked its driver. Startled, Hayes answered in the voice of her character. "You'd better buzz off, young man," she hissed. "I'm a killer!" By the time she realized what she had said, the young man had sped away, possibly cured of directing rude questions to strange women.

Hayes's next project found her teamed up with screen actor James Stewart. The two veteran stars staged a revival of *Harvey*, a 1944 hit comedy about a tipsy dreamer (Stewart), his dizzy sister (Hayes), and a six-foot rabbit (invisible). The production, called "more enjoyable than the original" by critic Brooks Atkinson, earned cheers for both its stars. Clive Barnes of the *New York Times* called Stewart "delightful and charismatic." Of Hayes, he wrote: "She is one of those actors—Laurence Olivier is another, for she keeps the grandest company—where to watch *how* she is doing something is almost as pleasurable as *what* she is doing." Scheduled for a six-week run, *Harvey* played an additional month to accommodate eager theatergoers.

Hayes had announced her retirement from the stage more than once, but each time she prepared to leave the theater, another new and exciting opportunity had presented itself. In 1971,

James Stewart and Hayes rehearse a scene from Harvey *in 1972. The Stewart-Hayes revival of Mary Chase's 1944 hit comedy, said critics, was even better than the original.*

when she made the step at last, it was dictated by her health. No matter how carefully they were cleaned, all theaters, with their heavy stage curtains, upholstered seats, and carpeted aisles, were thick with dust. Always susceptible to common house dust, Hayes had suffered several respiratory attacks over the years. She had learned to suppress her sneezes during performances, but her vulnerability had been an ongoing problem.

Now, during rehearsals for a 1971 production of Eugene O'Neill's tragic 1957 play, *Long Day's Journey Into Night*, dust struck again. When Hayes developed a hard, persistent cough, her doctors ordered her to leave the play or risk contracting pneumonia. At the age of 71, she knew the disease could kill her. But, ever the professional, she refused to abandon a project to which she had committed herself. Characteristically, she treated the situation with humor. "I was afraid if I didn't go on," she wrote later, "they'd say I was too old to remember my lines."

Hayes's final stage appearance proved one of her greatest triumphs. *Long Day's Journey Into Night* is a massive and complex work, presenting its interpreters with unusual challenges. Hayes's role, that of the drug-haunted mother of the fictionalized O'Neill family, is notoriously difficult to play. As Mary Tyrone, however, Hayes stunned reviewers. Gone were all traces of "cuteness"; vanished was the sunny, smiling Hayes familiar to several generations of theatergoers. As Tyrone, Hayes created a heartbreaking picture of a loving and intelligent woman helplessly rushing toward self-destruction. "I came as close as I ever wanted to complete fulfillment in my acting when I played Mary Tyrone," Hayes wrote later.

Walter Kerr, dean of Broadway's theater critics, agreed. Most actresses, he said, play Tyrone as doomed from the start, thus spoiling viewers' gradual discovery of her disintegration. Hayes, on the other hand, began the play as a self-confident, "nearly normal" wife

and mother, then slowly revealed the demons within herself. "Miss Hayes gained suspense to begin with and a heart-sinking sympathy when, inevitably, the foundation gives way," wrote Kerr. "The standing ovation she received was in order and not simply because she had spent a lifetime being Helen Hayes. It was Eugene O'Neill she was working for, first to last."

Hayes had been a working actress for 65 years. She would act for years to come, but with the close of *Long Day's Journey*, the final curtain had fallen on her stage career. From this point on, the First Lady of the American Theater would work only in films.

Because *Airport* had made Hayes popular with a new generation of moviegoers, producers began bombarding her with scripts for films and television shows. She appeared in a 1971 TV movie, *Do Not Fold, Spindle, or Mutilate*; in a 1972 episode of Lucille Ball's "Here's Lucy" show; and in a televised adaptation of the novel *Ghost Story*. Also in 1972, she and an old friend, actress Mildred Natwick, costarred in *The Snoop Sisters*, a made-for-TV movie that became a regular weekly series. Portraying a pair of aging mystery writers who set out to solve real-life murders, Hayes and Natwick earned critical praise. But the series,

Making her final stage appearance, Hayes pulls out all the stops as Mary Tyrone, the tragic heroine of Eugene O'Neill's Long Day's Journey into Night.

burdened with flat, unfunny scripts, failed to achieve a long run. Nevertheless, Hayes had no regrets about experimenting with the project. "I think now I've tried everything—except burlesque," said the 72-year-old actress, "and I don't think I'd be very good at that."

Still eager for new experiences, Hayes quickly accepted her next offer: to costar with a Volkswagen car in a new movie. The 1974 film, *Herbie Rides Again*, would be a sequel to Disney Studios' *The Love Bug*, an enormously successful screen comedy about a racing driver and his talking car. This time, Hayes would play opposite Herbie, the whimsical, independent-minded vehicle that she later called "the real star of the picture." Hayes liked the innocent "Herbie" comedies, and she also liked the idea of working for Disney, the studio where her actor son, James MacArthur, had built his early career. The year after she filmed *Herbie*, Hayes appeared with MacArthur in an episode of his TV series, "Hawaii Five-O."

For Hayes, a highlight of her television career arrived in 1977, when she appeared in *A Family Upside Down*. She agreed to the project, a film drama about the generation gap, largely because it gave her the chance to play opposite Fred Astaire. Originally famed for his brilliant dancing, Astaire had recently gained respect as a dramatic actor. Hayes, who had known Astaire casually for more than half a century, admired his skills but had never worked with him. "It's taken all these

Hayes gives her Herbie Rides Again *costar an affectionate pat. According to Hayes, the Volkswagen was "the real star" of the popular 1974 movie.*

years, but we finally made it, kid," said the 78-year-old Astaire to the 77-year-old Hayes. "I guess I'm glad it didn't happen any earlier, laddie," she responded with a laugh. "Because then I'd have had to be your dancing partner. And with these two left feet, that would be too much for you to bear!" The two veterans scored a smash in *A Family Upside Down*, which earned Astaire an Emmy Award.

Hayes kept on saying she was about to retire, but she kept on accepting new roles. In 1981 she appeared in *Murder is Easy*, the first of three television movies based on Agatha Christie mystery novels. Next came *A Caribbean Mystery*, in which Hayes played Christie's celebrated amateur detective, Miss Jane Marple. In the last of the film trio, *Murder with Mirrors*, Hayes shared the screen with Bette Davis and John Mills. *Murder is Easy* and *A Caribbean Mystery* had been greeted with polite but not dazzling reviews. *Murder with Mirrors* turned out to be another story: According to the TV ratings, more than 20 million people watched the 1985 movie, which had received glowing notices from British and American reviewers.

At first elated about the size of her audience, Hayes later found herself feeling sad about it. More people had seen her in what she called "a mediocre TV show" than had ever seen her during her 80 years on the stage. "All those plays, all those beautiful lines, all that shared intimacy with live patrons," she lamented, had reached only a tiny fraction of the viewers who had seen *Murder with Mirrors*. "Was this the way I wanted to be remembered?" she asked herself. Deciding she had reached "the breaking point" in her TV career, she called it quits. When her producer asked her to play Miss Marple again, she said no. "No more acting on stage, screen, or TV," said Hayes firmly. At the age of 84, actress Helen Hayes had finally retired.

But activist Helen Hayes was nowhere near retirement. She had already written three books: the inspirational

A Gift of Joy, in 1965; the autobiographical *On Reflection*, in 1968; and, with her friend Anita Loos, a book about New York City, *Twice Over Lightly*, in 1972. She planned to write more, and she did: Both *A Gathering of Hope* (1985) and *Our Best Years* (1986) elaborated on the pleasures of old age. In 1990, she produced a second volume of autobiography, *My Life in Three Acts*.

Hayes joins a 1979 Actors' Equity picket line in New York City. After her 1971 retirement from the stage, the actress found herself busier than ever.

Anita Loos and Helen Hayes autograph their 1972 book, Twice Over Lightly, *in a New York bookshop. Author of five earlier volumes, Hayes published a new autobiography in early 1990.*

As Hayes grew older, she turned her attention to the problems confronting other elderly people. In 1980, she began taping "The Best Years," a daily two-minute radio message aimed at aging Americans. In 1982, she addressed the United States Senate, advocating government support of home care for the elderly. "There I was, on the floor of the Senate at age 82," she recalled cheerfully, "making a big noise and telling everyone that my generation has got to be noticed." And she continued to make "a big noise," speaking in Congress, persuading large employers to hire the elderly, and traveling across the country to talk to other senior citizens. "Don't vegetate," she urged them. "Don't sit back and relax." Dur-

ing one lecture, she told a group of retired schoolteachers that opportunities should be available to all older people willing and able to work, not only to "well-known, white-haired actresses." Jobs, she said, "should be based on one thing and one thing alone, and that is who can handle the job best." Once again, an audience gave Helen Hayes a standing ovation.

Other ovations and honors continued to pour in. Hayes received the Kennedy Center Award and the Presidential Medal of Freedom; in her name, admirers established awards, scholarships, and hospital wings. When Haverstraw, New York, the town next to Nyack, built a new $38 million hospital, the community dedicated it to Hayes. And when Manhattan reconstruction plans called for demolition of the Helen Hayes Theatre, a brigade of furious stage and screen celebrities picketed West 46th Street. The protest failed, but Broadwayites made up for it by renaming the Little Theatre on West 44th Street. Speaking at the dedication of the new Helen Hayes Theatre, the actress said, "The theater has been my whole life. It has given me every great thing I ever had. I hope this theater will have many long runs and outlive me." But Hayes had no immediate plans to be outlived by anything: Having seen the 20th century in, she said, she intended to see it out.

On October 10, 1989, a galaxy of theatrical stars assembled at Manhattan's Algonquin Hotel. Here, New York's long-vanished glitterati had held court in the 1920s, sipping cocktails,

Florida representative Claude Pepper seats Hayes at a 1981 congressional hearing. The actress later spoke in support of home health-care programs for elderly Americans.

trading witticisms, and terrifying a young actress they dubbed "that awful little Helen." But in 1989, "little Helen" ruled the night. Diamonds glittering at her throat, the First Lady of the American Theater beamed as 200

103

At the age of 89, Hayes recommended staying interested in people and events. "Curiosity may have killed the cat," she said in her 1990 autobiography, "but it did all right by me."

friends raised champagne toasts to her 89th birthday. At Hayes's request, the party also celebrated a project close to her heart: the renovation of an old theater in her own hometown. She and her colleagues had organized a $4 million fund-raising drive to restore Nyack's century-old Tappan Zee Playhouse; now the work had neared completion.

Standing amid cascades of white roses and birthday presents, Hayes talked about the playhouse, scheduled to reopen in 1991 as the Helen Hayes–Tappan Zee Performing Arts Center. "A theater is a very good thing for any community," she told the cheering crowd. "I've been all over the country opening theaters for people, and I've finally come home to open one in my own community." Noting that the restored theater would present jazz, folk and chamber music, films, poetry readings, and plays, Hayes declared, "We're going to take Times Square to Nyack."

Between public appearances, Hayes spent most of her time in Nyack. Living at Pretty Penny with a companion, she followed the same habits she urged others to adopt: taking daily walks and swimming for exercise, entertaining friends, working in her garden, keeping in touch with her colleagues, and developing new projects. As she often told her audiences, "if you rest, you rust."

A Broadway star at the age of eight, a film performer even before the legendary Charlie Chaplin, a stage actress beloved by generations of theatergoers, Hayes made theatrical history. She was the first stage star to win an Academy Award, the first performer to win Oscars for both best actress and best supporting actress, the first actress to win a Tony Award, the first individual for whom two Broadway theaters were named. Hayes once described herself as "an ordinary woman who has led an extraordinary life." For most theater fans, however, the word "ordinary" has no place in a discussion of Helen Hayes.

"She radiated a sort of magic on the stage," wrote critic Brooks Atkinson in his theatrical history, *Broadway*. "She made the theater larger than life." Atkinson, who observed that "the relationship between actress and public became increasingly personal" over the years, said no audience had "been able to withhold itself from the unaffected star who began as Peaseblossom in *A Midsummer Night's Dream*." The critic noted that "Peaseblossom has only two lines in that play. One of them is her response to a question Bottom asks her. 'Ready,' she says. Miss Hayes has been ready all her life."

Talking to a reporter in the mid-1980s, Hayes said she thought today's women faced harder decisions than the women of her generation. "I don't know how I'd manage if I were a young woman starting a career and family today," she remarked. But after a short pause, she said firmly, "I guess I would do just as I did before. I would decide on what really mattered to me and fight for it all the way."

FURTHER READING

Atkinson, Brooks. *Broadway.* New York: Macmillan, 1985.

Barrow, Kenneth. *Helen Hayes, First Lady of the American Theatre.* New York: Doubleday, 1985.

Friedrich, Otto. *City of Nets: A Portrait of Hollywood in the 1940s.* New York: Harper & Row, 1986.

Hayes, Helen. *A Gathering of Hope.* New York: Doubleday, 1985.

Hayes, Helen, with Sandford Dody. *On Reflection: An Autobiography.* New York: M. Evans, 1968.

Hayes, Helen, with Lewis Funke. *A Gift of Joy.* New York: M. Evans, 1965.

Hayes, Helen, with Marion Gladney. *Our Best Years.* New York: Doubleday, 1986.

Hayes, Helen, with Katherine Hatch. *My Life in Three Acts.* New York: Harcourt Brace Jovanovich, 1990.

Hayes, Helen, and Anita Loos. *Twice Over Lightly: New York Then and Now.* New York: Harcourt Brace Jovanovich, 1972.

Loos, Anita. *Cast of Thousands.* New York: Grosset & Dunlap, 1977.

Mordden, Ethan. *The American Theatre.* New York: Oxford University Press, 1986.

Palmer, Edwin. *A History of Hollywood.* New York: Garland Publishing, 1978.

CHRONOLOGY

Oct. 10, 1900	Born Helen Hayes Brown in Washington, D.C.
1905	Makes stage debut as Peaseblossom in *A Midsummer Night's Dream*
1909	Appears in first Broadway show, *Old Dutch*
1910	Makes first movie, *Jean and the Calico Doll*
1914	Appears in *The Prodigal Husband* with John Drew
1917	Starts regional tour in *Pollyanna*
1918	Appears in *Dear Brutus* with William Gillette
1920	Opens in Boston, then New York City, in *Bab*
1927	Stars in *Coquette*
1928	Marries playwright Charles MacArthur
1930	Gives birth to daughter, Mary MacArthur
1931	Makes two movies, *The Sin of Madelon Claudet* and *Arrowsmith*
1932	Wins Academy Award for role of Madelon; costars with Gary Cooper in *A Farewell to Arms*
1933	Appears on Broadway in *Mary of Scotland*
1937	Adopts son, James; opens in *Victoria Regina*
1940	Father, Frank Brown, dies
1946	Hayes appears in *Happy Birthday*; wins Tony Award
1948	Appears in *The Glass Menagerie* in London
1949	Daughter dies of polio
1950	Hayes makes first television appearance
1952	Campaigns for public acceptance of polio vaccine
1953	Mother, Catherine Hayes Brown, dies
1956	Husband, Charles MacArthur, dies; Hayes appears in film *Anastasia*; returns to Catholic church
1957	Stars in *Time Remembered* on Broadway
1958	Appears in Eugene O'Neill's *A Touch of the Poet*
1961	Makes theater tour for U.S. State Department
1966	Joins Phoenix-APA repertory company in Manhattan
1969	Stars in TV's *Arsenic and Old Lace*
1970	Appears in film *Airport*; wins second Academy Award
1971	Appears in O'Neill's *Long Day's Journey Into Night*; retires from theater
1974	Appears in film *Herbie Rides Again*
1982	Addresses U.S. Senate about problems of the elderly
1984	Appears in television movie *Murder With Mirrors*; retires as actress
1990	Publishes fifth book, *My Life in Three Acts*

INDEX

INDEX

Mary Kittredge is a novelist and biographer who lives in Connecticut. She was educated at Trinity College in Hartford and the University of California Medical Center in San Francisco. Her writing awards include the Ruell Crompton Tuttle Essay Prize and the Mystery Writers of America Robert L. Fish Award for best first short-mystery fiction of 1986. She has written several young-adult books on health and is also the author of *Marc Antony* and *Frederick the Great* in Chelsea House's WORLD LEADERS—PAST & PRESENT series and *Jane Addams* in Chelsea House's AMERICAN WOMEN OF ACHIEVEMENT series.

❖   ❖   ❖

Matina S. Horner is president emerita of Radcliffe College and associate professor of psychology and social relations at Harvard University. She is best known for her studies of women's motivation, achievement, and personality development. Dr. Horner serves on several national boards and advisory councils, including those of the National Science Foundation, Time Inc., and the Women's Research and Education Institute. She earned her B.A. from Bryn Mawr College and Ph.D. from the University of Michigan, and holds honorary degrees from many colleges and universities, including Mount Holyoke, Smith, Tufts, and the University of Pennsylvania.